(Continued from front flap)

This book was originally prepared as a data paper for the Eleventh International Conference of the Institute of Pacific Relations, held in India in October, 1950. It has since been revised and a chapter has been added carrying the story through the summer of 1951 and discussing the issues raised by Communist China's intervention in the Korean war.

"A clarifying narrative notable for its balance and perspective . . . the reader will also find an excellent summary of issues precipitated by the MacArthur dismissal."—*Far Eastern Quarterly*

THE AUTHOR

Harold M. Vinacke, Professor of Political Science at the University of Cincinnati, is one of America's leading authorities on the Far East and its relations with the United States. He has taught at Nankai University, Tientsin, and during World War II he was a specialist on Japan for the Office of War Information. He is the author of *A History of the Far East in Modern Times* and other books.

STANFORD UNIVERSITY PRESS
Stanford, California

THE UNITED STATES
AND THE FAR EAST

1945 – 1951

THE INSTITUTE OF PACIFIC RELATIONS

THE UNITED STATES AND THE FAR EAST
1945-1951

Harold M. Vinacke
Professor of Political Science
University of Cincinnati

*Published under the auspices of the
American Institute of Pacific Relations, Inc.*

STANFORD UNIVERSITY PRESS
Stanford, California
GEOFFREY CUMBERLEGE: OXFORD UNIVERSITY PRESS
London
1952

First printing, March 1952

Second printing, July 1953

Library of Congress Catalog Card Number: 52-1172

STANFORD UNIVERSITY PRESS
Stanford, California

GEOFFREY CUMBERLEGE: OXFORD UNIVERSITY PRESS
London

THE BAKER AND TAYLOR COMPANY
55 FIFTH AVENUE, NEW YORK 3

HENRY M. SNYDER & COMPANY
440 FOURTH AVENUE, NEW YORK 16

W. S. HALL & COMPANY
457 MADISON AVENUE, NEW YORK 22

Preface

The dismissal of General MacArthur precipitated a national debate on issues of American Far Eastern policy which in scope and bitterness has seldom been surpassed in American history. While the controversy was initially concerned with the wisdom or unwisdom of certain recommendations made by General MacArthur for the conduct of the war in Korea, it soon broadened into a reexamination of the whole conduct of United States policy in Asia since the end of World War II. If the basic aim of American foreign policy is peace and security, it appeared to many that these goals were much farther off than they had been in 1945, and that the United States was losing strong friends in Asia faster than it was making them. Where lay the fault—in errors of judgment by the Administration responsible for the conduct of our policy, in domestic critics who had tied the Administration's hands, in Russian machinations, or in revolutionary forces in Asia beyond the reach of foreign control?

In order to judge such questions it is necessary to place current issues in their proper perspective, by examining the record of United States policy in the Far East since 1945, against the background of earlier history, and in relation to the equally complex problems which the United States has faced in Europe. The present compact summary by Professor Vinacke will, it is hoped, aid the thoughtful citizen in appraising the grave issues which confront this country today. This study is neither a defense of the Administration's record nor an attack upon it. It is an account of the main events and issues by a distinguished political scientist, most of whose life has been spent in close study of events in Asia and their relation to America.

The American Institute of Pacific Relations, which for twenty-six years has been engaged in promoting the scientific study and non-partisan discussion of Asian questions, presents this short survey not as an addition to the "great debate" but as an aid to public understanding of the issues involved. Since the American IPR as an organization does not express opinions or advocate policies, the author alone is responsible for the views expressed in this volume.

This study was originally prepared as a data paper for the eleventh international conference of the Institute of Pacific Relations, held at Lucknow, India, in October 1950. It has since been revised slightly and enlarged by the addition of a chapter carrying the story through the summer of 1951, and discussing the issues raised by Communist China's intervention in the Korean war.

W. L. Holland
Executive Vice Chairman,
American Institute of Pacific Relations

New York
October, 1951

Contents

1. *Introduction: The Importance of Europe in United States Policy*

The development and application of American foreign policy were fundamentally changed by the antecedents, the circumstances, and the outcome of World War II. It had come to be recognized that the United States could not continue to follow its traditional policy of non-participation in European politics in time of so-called peace, with its correlative of neutrality in the event of war. The abandonment of the idea of neutrality as a normal reaction to "foreign" (i.e. European) quarrels, which was forced by the antecedents, as well as the circumstances, of World War II, developed a different appreciation of the role of force in international politics. This new point of view revealed itself initially in some of the provisions of the United Nations Charter. But the preoccupation with power as an instrument of politics came fully to the surface only with the perception of the fact that the war had left the world with only two major centers of power, the United States and the Soviet Union, without agreement between them as to the uses to which, from the standpoint of international relations, power should be put.

With the acceptance of the United Nations Charter it had been assumed that the major powers would cooperate in the establishment of the conditions of peace and in the maintenance of the arrangements of peace, once agreed upon. Within this assumption were two others: first, that it was with respect mainly to Germany and Japan that safeguards against military aggression had to be erected and second,

1

that British and French power would be revived rapidly enough so that they could play the major role in European politics which had once been theirs. The role of the United States, from the power standpoint, could then be comparable to that previously played by Britain in the maintenance of the European and world balance of power. This role could be played within the framework of the United Nations organization.

Instead of these assumptions being verified, however, Soviet policy in eastern and southeastern Europe, and later in relation to Germany, brought the United States to the view that the primary objective must be the erection of barriers to Soviet expansionism. This view was expressed first in the Truman Doctrine of containment of Communism and then in the Marshall Plan, with its extension into the concept of a Western European and North Atlantic regional defense system. Thus within a relatively short time United States policy had come to involve

"(1) continuous participation in the affairs of Europe, through economic aid, support of projects for a Western European Union, and assurance to the countries of the West that the United States will assist them in the case of aggression; (2) opposition all over the globe to Russia and Communism, implemented in Europe by economic and military measures designed to contain both the national ambitions of the Russians and the influence of native Communists; and (3) actions and projects within the framework of the United Nations, extending beyond the boundaries of Europe into other continents, but having repercussions on European developments—notably plans for the realization of President Truman's Point Four."[1]

In fact, however, in the initial postwar years the major emphasis of American foreign policy was on Europe. It was there that American power and American resources were primarily committed to the containment of Soviet power. Other continents received only "such attention and resources as [the United States] could spare after filling European requirements" since American "military, economic, and technical resources, although exceeding those of any other contemporary nation, are not boundless."[2]

This preoccupation with Europe was due to accumulating evidences of British weakness as a world power as well as to evidences of Soviet expansionism. This caused the United States to assume responsibilities in the Mediterranean and in the Middle East which Britain otherwise might have continued to bear. It gradually became apparent that the possibility of sharing the burden of "containment of Russia and Communism" in non-European areas as well as in Europe depended upon a revival of the power of Britain, and of other Western European states. But this, in turn, necessitated American concern for conditions, especially in Southeast Asia, which militated against Western European recovery. The changed conditions in Southeast Asia were the result of the war.

2. Southeast Asia in United States Policy

Before World War II Southeast Asia had been stabilized on a colonial basis so far as international rivalry and conflict were concerned. Nationalism had begun to appear as a force with which the colonial powers would ultimately have to deal. But Western imperialism, against which nationalism was a natural reaction, had become recessive rather than aggressive. American colonial policy, long verbally directed toward self-government in the Philippines, moved toward early Filipino independence with the Tydings-McDuffie Act, followed in 1936 by the establishment of the Commonwealth government. This carried with it a commitment to grant political independence after ten years. At the other end of the colonial area, the Government of Burma Act of 1937 promised self-government and ultimate Commonwealth status for Burma. Siam, before World War II the only independent state in the region, was controlled by nationalist elements. Under the impact of nationalist parties Dutch colonial policy was slightly modified. And nationalist parties had appeared in French Indo-China.

Nevertheless, all the surface indications were that the colonial powers would be able to adjust their policies to the new pressures in terms of their own judgment as to the timing, the method, and the extent of the immediate adjustments required. The United States acquiesced in this view. This acquiescence resulted from the United States' ability in general to supply its needs for rubber, tin, and other raw

4

materials from the area by competitive operations made possible by the generally nonrestrictive trade policies of the colonial powers. Its interest, in other words, was in the conditions of trade access to the production of the colonial area. Beyond this, but for the same reason, it was interested in the maintenance of political stability, since production depends upon order. Thus, as long as the colonial power showed the ability to rule and as long as its commercial policies were not unduly restrictive, the United States seemed prepared to acquiesce in the continuation of colonialism even though its Philippine policy represented a departure from it.

The growth of nationalism, however, had begun to raise questions about the colonial power's ability to rule and maintain order except as it prepared to introduce measures of self-government. The supporters of the American Philippine policy saw in that policy an example which the other colonial powers should be encouraged to follow. But generally speaking the legalities of the situation were held to require acquiescence in the policies followed by each metropolitan country for its own colonies, except where those policies directly and adversely affected the economic interests of the United States. As long as such acquiescence continued, Southeast Asia was essentially withdrawn from the conflicts of international politics.

(a) Effects of the War on Southeast Asia

The war changed the entire Southeast Asia picture. Japan temporarily displaced Britain in Burma and Malaya, the Dutch in the Netherlands Indies, and the Americans in the Philippines. Occupied France had to accept the manipulation of the French regime in Indo-China to serve Japan's interests. The government of Thailand, although allied with Japan, in effect lost its independence. Japan's proclaimed purpose was to create a "Greater Asia Co-Prosperity Sphere," tying the entire colonial area as well as China and Manchuria into an empire with Japan as the processing and exchange center. Had this purpose been realized, an East and Southeast Asia regional political economy would have replaced an area of separate countries with disparate interests and independent policy problems. The war, however, made this impossible of achievement even within the framework of Japanese policy. Submarine and air operations cut Japan off from effectual economic contact with the occupied countries, so that each was required to live by its own resources. In most Southeast Asian countries production had been developed on an export commodity basis rather than on a basis of diversification designed to maintain relative self-sufficiency. With normal markets cut off the effect of the Japanese occupation was not merely to increase poverty and hardship but also to reduce production and to produce economic disorganization and dislocation. Thus the reoccupying colonial powers attempted to reestablish their authority in countries which were immediate economic liabilities rather than assets, since each required extensive expenditures for economic rehabilitation and reconstruction as well as to restore order.

Aside from this, the net effect of the Japanese occupation was to strengthen the nationalist demand for self-government and independence, while supplying some of the means for gaining independence. Anticipating defeat in some cases, and hoping to transfer some of the responsibility for defense to national regimes in others, the Japanese created "independent" governments in the Philippines and Burma, and began to establish some of the institutions of self-government in Indonesia and Malaya. In these countries, and also in Indo-China, furthermore, reaction to Japanese maladministration stimulated nationalist resistance movements which in some instances had connections with the Japanese-sponsored governments. In either case, the effect was twofold: (1) it developed a more mature and experienced leadership with nationalist aspirations, and (2) it put arms, for the first time, in the hands of those seeking either a larger measure of self-government or actual independence. The circumstances of the Japanese surrender in the various countries, except for the Philippines, also increased the quantity of arms available to the forces controlled by nationalist leaders.

All of this changed the problems of reestablishing the prewar status. During the war the colonial powers assumed that the Japanese would have aroused sufficient hostility to themselves so that the former rulers would be welcomed back as liberators under circumstances permitting them to determine the extent and rate of change in their prewar policies. During the war both the British and the Dutch indicated an intention to develop their policies toward self-government. But it was to be their judgment which would determine change, and that judgment would be exercised only after the *status quo ante* 1941 had been reestablished. The French, after the liberation of France, wrote into the constitution of the Fourth Republic the conception of the French Union to replace that of the Empire, but its meaning was not clear to the people of Indo-China, nor did it seem to some of their leaders to go far enough toward independence.

The unexpected consequence of the Japanese occupation of Southeast Asia was to require each metropolitan country either to negotiate with new governments the conditions of its return or to apply sufficient force against its subjects, rather than the Japanese, to restore its authority. Except possibly in Malaya (where the circumstances were exceptional), active hostility was shown to the colonial power to the extent to which it refused to develop its policy, not from the status of 1941 but from that established by the Japanese in the last weeks of their rule. Instead of Japan's surrender introducing a new period of stability and order in Southeast Asia, and

Asia.* It is, however, essential to emphasize the fact that war and postwar developments made it necessary for the United States to think of Southeast Asia, from the policy standpoint, in terms somewhat dissociated from and independent of Europe and European policy. Before the war this area, with its relatively stable relationships, had not for some time been a serious problem, and therefore had not required separate policy decisions. Since the war it has joined China as one of the world's problem areas. Unlike China, however, it presents a series of country problems, each requiring separate definition and a separate policy, except as there develops such a common spool on which to wind American policy as that presently represented by Communism. In this respect the policy is not strictly a Far Eastern policy but represents a regional application of world policy.

* See Lawrence S. Finkelstein, *American Policy in Southeast Asia* (New York: Institute of Pacific Relations, 1950).

3. China in United States Policy

(a) Prewar Background

Because of their colonial character, the countries of Southeast Asia and the Southwest Pacific were ordinarily not viewed as being exclusively or primarily within the area of American Far Eastern policy. Even apart from them, it is difficult to find a distinct overall American Far Eastern policy. What was usually referred to in prewar days as United States Far Eastern policy was China policy, together with a regional application of the general principles on which the foreign policies of the United States were erected. These may be generalized as involving: (1) an attempt to secure for Americans equality of competitive opportunity in commerce and in investment; (2) respect for and an interest in seeing maintained the territorial and administrative integrity and the political independence of the states in the Far East as well as throughout the world; and (3) a willingness to give up special rights which had been secured, provided that did not put the United States or Americans in an unequal position vis-à-vis other outside states or their nationals. It might be added that the United States insisted upon respect for such special rights or privileges as were embodied in the terms of treaties until the treaty provisions had been changed by agreement.

Within this framework of principle, as far as American policy and actions were concerned, Japan emerged from her

11

period of seclusion under the same general treaty limitations as those imposed on China but was able fairly quickly to establish herself as a fully independent state with as complete control of her national policies as any Western state. The soundness of the resulting situation, as measured by American interests, was shown in the expansion of American trade with Japan and in the failure of Japan to become a center of international rivalry and conflict. It was where Japanese policy with respect to other states in the Far East, notably China, carried a threat to the principle of equality of competitive access and to the independence and integrity of other states that an independent Japan became involved as a center of conflict.

From this standpoint, Korea first became involved in difficulty and found her status threatened by Japan and Russia. Ultimately (in 1910) she became a part of the Japanese Empire by formal annexation. This was accomplished as a result of two wars, in relation to both of which the United States officially stood apart as a declared neutral.

The principal center of international rivalry and conflict in the Far East after the first Sino-Japanese war was China. Within China the area of acute conflict was Manchuria. And it was with respect to China that the above special definitions of substantive American policy were made. So far as success was met in making effective the principles (and that success was only partial even before 1931) it was because first Russian and then Japanese policy was restrained by the interests and actions of other states than the United States. In effect, up to 1931 there was at least a semblance of a balance of power in the Far East which operated to prevent any one state from following its own self-determined lines of interest in China. It was Japan which prevented the establishment of Russian control in Manchuria in the war of 1904-1905. Japan, however, was successful because of the assurance which the Anglo-Japanese Agreement gave her of British support and because of American financial assistance. The conditions of peace formulated at Portsmouth were viewed with some satisfaction by the American government because it was assumed that Russia, left in North Manchuria, would restrain Japan in South Manchuria, and vice versa. It was also assumed that, given the references to the Open Door in the Portsmouth Treaty, while Japan had succeeded to the Russian rights and interests in southern Manchuria the use which she would make of them would be consistent with American interests and would follow the lines of American policy marked out by Secretary of State John Hay. The test of the validity of the first assumption was immediately presented as Japan indicated an intention to succeed to Russian policy as well as to her rights, and this invalidated the second assumption. The test proved the first assumption also not correct.

Consequently, American policy came to emphasize maintaining the integrity of China in Manchuria against Japan. The means which the Taft administration sought to employ were financial, involving the introduction of American capital into Manchuria for railway construction. Concurrently a place was sought for American capital in the construction of railways in China. But here it was again shown that the attainment of the ends of American policy depended upon securing support from others with a similar interest. The search for this support took the United States to London, Paris, Berlin, and St. Petersburg. It met with limited success, partly because of the delicate web of agreements woven in anticipation of the first World War, and partly because the United States was not prepared to offer a sufficient return to Britain for the loss which she would face by alienating her ally, Japan. Nevertheless an element of restraint was introduced into Japanese policy by the possibility of losing the good will of European powers, as well as that of the United

States, if she were to go too far too fast and with too much disregard of the interests of other states.

World War I for the first time gave Japan a relatively free hand, except for the United States, in developing her China policies. The Twenty-one Demands on China in 1915 indicated the direction of her policies. However, uncertainty as to her long-term ability after the war to maintain absolute predominance in the Far East against European objections, as well as the American reaction to the Demands, tempered Japan's short-run policy. It was this uncertainty rather than the United States' declaration of nonrecognition of any changes violating American treaty rights or vested interests which gave a measure of support to American policy. And it was the wartime growth of American power, coupled with European support at the Washington Conference, which brought about international acceptance of American policy for China.

The Washington Conference treaties were, however, designed to set the pattern for the future and not to give an *ex post facto* application to policy so far as vested interests were concerned. Consequently the changes made in the *status quo* of 1900 adverse to China's independence and territorial and administrative integrity and to the Open Door became, with some exceptions, part of a new *status quo*. To this extent, certainly, it must be recognized that the Washington Conference agreements failed to implement the historic American policy. They did, however, restate it on the basis of international agreement, and at the same time revealed consistency in point of view in the formulation of American interests and objectives.

Consistency was also shown in the approach to the problem of implementation of policy. The arms limitation and non-fortification agreements entered into at the Washington Conference were designed in part to assure Japan against successful attack by any single power, including the United States, thus in effect putting her on her honor to observe the limitations which the Nine Power Treaty set upon her China policy. This indicated an American intention to rely on legal and moral restraints rather than on physical power to secure respect for international engagements. It was also anticipated that the balance of power, reestablished at the end of the European war, would help to implement the Washington Conference agreements. But no firm commitment was entered into which would put power behind the Washington Conference system.

(b) American Policy from 1931 to 1941

The system was put to the test in and after 1931, following the September Manchurian Incident. This Incident also tested the entire mechanism constructed after World War I to maintain international peace and security. Especially in the United States, this mechanism had come to be construed as operable on the premise that international public opinion would enforce the observance of international commitments. In fact, however, the collective condemnation of Japan's use of force to attain her objectives proved insufficient to change her Manchurian policies, as did Secretary Stimson's declaration, ultimately concurred in by the League States, of non-recognition of changes made by methods proscribed under such international instruments as the Kellogg-Briand Pact. This was a distinct American initiative, in contrast with the previous policy of supporting the efforts made at Geneva to settle the difficulty.

Non-recognition, however, did not serve to introduce restraint into Japanese policy any more than did the public condemnation expressed by other countries. "At present," wrote Ambassador Grew,[3] "the moral obloquy of the world is a negligible force in Japan. Far from serving to modify the determination of the Japanese, it merely tends to strengthen it." By 1937 it should have become clear that national policies of force could be modified only by the development and use of equivalent or of superior power. This conclusion had been drawn by the time of the Lukouchiao incident in North China by the Chinese government, supported by the pressure of nationalist opinion. Then for the first time in her recent history China sought, in the war of national resistance, to maintain her sovereignty and territorial integrity by her own military means, at least long enough to find allies whose power would be sufficient to overcome that of Japan.

The initial indications were that there would be no deviation from the traditional American policy, in spite of Secretary of State Hull's statement of July 16, 1937 that "Any situation in which armed hostilities are in progress or are threatened is a situation wherein rights and interests of all nations either are or may be seriously affected. There can be no serious hostilities anywhere in the world which will not one way or another affect interests or rights or obligations of this country." This statement of interest was followed by a statement of policy summarized by Secretary Hull as follows:

> "I then stated what we advocated: national and international self-restraint; abstinence by all nations from use of force in pursuit of policy and from interference in the internal affairs of other nations; adjustment of international problems by peaceful negotiation and agreement; faithful observance of international agreements; modification of treaties, when necessary, by orderly processes in a spirit of mutual helpfulness and accommodation; respect by all nations for the rights of others and performance of established obligations; revitalizing and strengthening of international law; economic se-

curity and stability the world over; lowering or removing excessive trade barriers; effective equality
of commercial opportunity and treatment; limitation and reduction of armaments. . . . 'We avoid
entering into alliances or entangling commitments,
but we believe in cooperative effort by peaceful
and practicable means in support of the principles
hereinbefore stated.' "[4]

Japan, whose actions had called forth the statement of
principles, subscribed to them but without making any change
in her policies. Consequently more importance must be attached to the statement as to how the United States proposed
to implement them than to the principles themselves as re-
statements of substantive policy. And on the procedural as
well as the substantive side, there is reaffirmation, against the
evidence of the years 1931-1937, of the efficacy of persuasion
at the time when the argument had already been transferred
from the council table to the battlefield.

One of the inhibiting factors in implementing American
diplomatic policy was the unwillingness to engage in joint
action, as distinguished from "cooperative effort," to restore
the peace. Joint action with France and the United States was
proposed by the British on July 20, 1937. This was declined by
Secretary Hull on three grounds:

"One was that it would create the impression in
Tokyo that the major Western nations were bringing pressure to bear on Japan. This would only
accentuate the crisis; the Japanese military could
use it to strengthen their own position and to in-
flame the populace against us. The second was that
if there was to be any joint action, it should be by all
of the nations having an interest in the Far East, or,
better still, by all of the peaceful nations of the

world, and not merely by two or three. The third was that anything resembling joint action with Britain inevitably aroused the fears and animosity of the isolationist elements in the United States.

"Moreover, I seriously doubted whether any joint action, unless it embraced a real show of force, backed by an intention to use force if necessary, would be of any avail. And I was certain that neither Great Britain, distracted by developments in Europe, nor the United States, unprepared psychologically and militarily, had any thought of employing force."[5]

American unwillingness to use force to implement policy had already been shown in the new neutrality legislation, designed to keep the United States out of war by the sacrifice of rights which it had previously sought to establish through the international law of neutrality. This, so far as Europe was concerned, was also expressive of the isolationism which Secretary Hull felt would be stirred to hostility by joint action with Britain. Neutrality and isolationist sentiment resulted in such a reaction to President Roosevelt's Chicago "Quarantine" address as to indicate that Secretary Hull's fears of American psychological unreadiness to consider using force to implement policy were not unwarranted.

Within the limits thus set, while others sought to induce American leadership to restrain Japan by indicating a readiness to follow, the United States could only back away from taking a real initiative. This was shown in its relationship to the Brussels Conference, which represented the final general "cooperative effort by peaceful and practicable means" to bring Japan back within the limits of "international morality" as defined in her treaty commitments.

After the failure of the Brussels Conference the United

States, as well as the European states, sought to minimize the consequences to its own nationals of hostilities between Japan and China. The method employed was that of diplomatic representations, "designed to produce two consequences. One was reparation for damage actually done. The other was the avoidance of future action which would inflict injury on the foreigner and necessitate further demands for reparation."[6] In making representations, the Hull policy continued to be, at the most, that of parallel or concurrent action with other interested or affected states. The substitution of national for international pressures met with some success in specific cases but did not produce any fundamental modification of Japanese policy.

On the contrary, while the "China Affair" could be viewed as a struggle between China and Japan exclusively during the first eighteen months, after the fall of Hankow in October 1938 it assumed more and more the added character of a struggle between the Western powers and Japan. This was a natural consequence of Japan's moves to consolidate her position in the occupied eastern areas of China. These moves involved action against Western rights and interests and restrictions on Western trade. Consequently, the United States commenced to shift "from defense of particular interests back to insistence on modification of Japanese policy in the direction of respect for the principle of equality of opportunity."[7] The Japanese government, however, by this time had begun to formulate as its policy the creation of a "new order in East Asia" to replace the Washington Conference system. This was ultimately enlarged into the "Greater East Asia Co-Prosperity Sphere" conception. Consequently, from 1939 to the end of 1941 the underlying issue remained posed as that between establishment of the traditional American China and Far Eastern policy and the policy of the closed regional political economy of Japan.

While Britain and France associated themselves with the American point of view, developments in Europe even before the outbreak of war materially reduced their ability to play positive roles in the Far East. After May 1940, only the United States and the Soviet Union had the power to act. The latter, however, concentrated its attention on expansion into eastern Europe and sought to secure its position against Japan by the neutrality pact of April 13, 1941, although it did give assistance to China which was important in enabling that country to maintain its resistance to Japan. Thus, although it had been giving more assistance to China against Japan than had come from other Western sources, and had been apparently on the brink of war against Japan from time to time, the Soviet Union made it clear that its immediate policy was exclusively the defense of the Soviet Far East. This forced the United States to acquiesce in Japan's "new order" or to find ways and means, largely by itself, of preventing its establishment.

The means employed were: (1) increased financial assistance to China, including lend-lease aid after 1941; (2) restrictions on the export of war materials to Japan, although the restrictions were initially justified in terms of the requirements of the American defense program rather than as a measure directed overtly against Japan; and (3) termination of the Commercial Treaty with Japan, and, in the summer of 1941, the freezing of Japanese assets within American jurisdiction. Up to the issuance of the "freezing order" the American reactions to Japan's actions had been kept technically within the framework of the new neutrality legislation. But American opinion, cultivated by the administration, had moved steadily away from insistence on "neutrality" to acceptance of a policy of "non-belligerency." It was ready for a more positive reaction by the time Japan had begun to extend her pressure into Southeast Asia and Indonesia.

In the conversations carried on, at the request of Japan, during 1941, it soon became clear that no basis of agreement could be found. Secretary Hull defined (April 16, 1941) four principles upon which any agreement would have to be founded. These summarized the historic American policy. The Japanese proposals of May 12, which it had been agreed should serve as the basis for the negotiations, provided they were founded on the Hull principles, were designed to commit the United States to the support of Japan. The prolonged conversations had revealed no willingness on either side to modify its fundamental position by the time when the American government sent its reply, on November 26, to the final Japanese proposal, defining the conditions of a temporary agreement. Thus the United States was finally compelled, as a result of the attack on Pearl Harbor, to attempt to implement its Far Eastern, or China, policy by military means.

(c) Evolution and Application of American Policy Toward China During World War II

One aspect of the China policy of the United States has been disregarded in the foregoing discussion. This was the American attitude toward the treaties which, from the middle of the nineteenth century, put China in a position of inequality with other states in the exercise of its sovereignty. The nineteenth-century treaty system involving extraterritoriality, treaty controls of China's tariff, and maintenance of foreign residential areas in some of China's cities, had been in process of revision in the direction of equality but the process had not been completed when Japan began to intensify her pressures in China. When the Nationalists assumed control of China's government one of their objectives was treaty revision. This had been promised conditionally at the Washington Conference and some steps toward revision had been taken by 1928. The United States position was that rights would be given up as it could be shown that changes had been made in China which made them no longer necessary. The Chinese Nationalists, when they assumed power, pressed for immediate revision and proposed to terminate the treaties unilaterally if the Western states and Japan were not willing immediately to negotiate new treaties. Under this pressure revision was accepted in principle. The intensification of Japanese pressure in and after 1931, however, redirected the emphasis of the Nanking government. Thus the extraterritorial treaties still remained in force when the war broke out.

An immediate effect of the entrance of the United States into the war was to make it an ally of China. This led to a reexamination of the relationship between the two countries and, in effect, hastened the conclusion of the negotiations intermittently carried on during the nineteen-thirties. The United States and China had entered into active negotiations in 1930 looking toward the relinquishment of American extraterritorial rights in China. These discussions were far advanced when in 1931 they were suspended as a consequence of the Japanese military occupation of Manchuria. The United States was giving renewed favorable considerations to the question of proceeding toward a relinquishment of extraterritorial jurisdiction in 1937, when Japan commenced its undeclared war by invading North China and subsequently Central and South China.

"From the Japanese invasion of China in July 1937 until the outbreak of war between the United States and Japan in December 1941, the extraterritorial system operated to the advantage of the United States, China, and the other countries opposed to Japanese aggressive activities, by providing protection for recognized treaty rights which the Japanese effort at monopoly violated. Although conditions did not favor taking active steps toward relinquishment of extraterritorial rights in China, the United States policy remained firm that such steps should be taken as soon as practicable."[8]

It did not, however, seem practicable to take the necessary steps immediately upon the outbreak of the Pacific war. "While the United Nations were suffering serious military reverses in the Far East it was felt that any action toward relinquishment of extraterritorial jurisdiction in China would have been interpreted widely as a gesture of weakness."[9] Treaty revision was, however, not too long delayed, a new treaty renouncing extraterritorial rights being signed on January 11, 1943. This was followed by an act, signed by the President on December 17, 1943, which

"repealed the Chinese exclusion laws, established an annual Chinese immigration quota, and made legally admitted Chinese eligible to naturalization as American citizens. The enactment of this legislation had been specifically recommended by President Roosevelt in order to 'correct an historic mistake' and give 'additional proof that we regard China not only as a partner in waging war but that we shall regard her as a partner in days of peace.' "[10]

These moves were designed to put China on a footing of legal equality among her allies. They also indicated an intention on the part of the United States to build up China as a potential Great Power in the family of nations. This process was carried further in planning for the creation of the United Nations and crystallized in the elevation of China to permanent membership on the Security Council, with the right of veto, on an equal status with the United States, the Soviet Union, Britain, and France. There was the same implication in the Cairo Declaration, which established as one of the purposes of the war the restoration to China of Manchuria, Formosa, and the Pescadores islands, thus giving her the territorial status of 1894.

The condition of China at this time, however, made her status as a "partner in days of peace" as well as in war one of assumption rather than fact. Before she could change her role from that of "problem country" to that of a stabilizing force in the politics of the Far East, it would be necessary not only to win the war against Japan but also to bring about internal unity and peace under a strong central government capable of undertaking the necessary rehabilitation and reconstruction of the national economy. American national policy, consequently, began to be directed toward that end. The policy formulated was based upon the idea that the various contending forces could be drawn together within a democratic framework of government. These contending forces were primarily the Kuomintang, which controlled the National Government, and the Communist Party, which governed the Northwest Border and had numerous local regimes responding to its authority in North China and in Central China within the Japanese occupied area. The problem as then defined was that of bringing the Communist regime and its military forces under the effective control of the National Government, thus unifying China. The method used to solve it was to negotiate the conditions of participation of the Communist Party in that government.

(d) China's Internal Problem

The initial approaches to a solution of the problem were made during the war. They were made primarily for short-run war purposes but they established the framework within which postwar policy was developed and applied. The peculiarities of the situation in China during and at the end of the war were of obvious importance in shaping American policy. These must be summarized at this point.

The first of these peculiarities was that the recognized government of China, with and through which relations had to be carried on, was virtually indistinguishable from the Kuomintang, one of the two parties contending for power. The Communist Party, however, had equally exclusive power in the part of China under its control. It had not, however, secured recognition as the government of its part of China. In other words, the fiction had been maintained that China was an entity with only one government through which it carried on its foreign relations. Because of this the United States could not, with propriety, approach the Communists directly, but only through the medium of the National Government and within limits set by it. In other words, it found itself inhibited from acting as the mediator between two legally equal parties. This put it in an anomalous position from the start in its endeavor to assist in negotiating an agreement between the Kuomintang-controlled government and the Communists which would bring the latter into the government.

A second peculiarity in the immediate situation was that while the United States could approach the Communists only under the auspices of the National Government, and while those approaches were made with a view to strengthening the government for war purposes as well as to create the conditions of postwar unity, the advices from China had begun to be to the effect that there had been such deterioration in the morale and effectiveness of the government that its position was becoming hopeless. Thus, as early as June 20, 1944,[11] the view was expressed that:

⌐ "The position of the Kuomintang and the Generalissimo is weaker than it has been for the past ten years.

"China faces economic collapse. This is causing disintegration of the army and the government's administrative apparatus. It is one of the chief ⌐causes of growing political unrest. The Generalissimo is losing the support of a China which, by unity in the face of violent aggression, found a new and unexpected strength during the first two years of the war with Japan. Internal weaknesses are becoming accentuated and there is taking place a reversal of the process of unification.

"1. Morale is low and discouragement widespread. There is a general feeling of hopelessness.

"2. The authority of the Central Government is weakening in the areas away from the larger cities. . . .

"3. The governmental and military structure is being permeated and demoralized from top to bottom by corruption, unprecedented in scale. . . .

"4. The intellectual and salaried classes, who have suffered the most heavily from inflation, are in ⌐danger of liquidation. The academic groups suffer not only the attrition and demoralization of economic stress; the weight of years of political control and repression is robbing them of the intellectual vigor and leadership they once had. . . .

⌐ "9. The Kuomintang is losing the respect and support of the people by its selfish policies and its ⌐refusal to heed progressive criticism. It seems unable to revivify itself with fresh blood, and its unchanging leadership shows a growing ossification and loss of a sense of reality. . . "

On the other hand, the Communists were reported to be in quite a different position.

> "The Chinese Communists are so strong between the Great Wall and the Yangtze that they can now look forward to the postwar control of at least North China. They may also continue to hold not only those parts of the Yangtze valley which they now dominate but also new areas in Central and South China. The Communists have fallen heir to these new areas by a process, which has been operating for seven years, whereby Chiang Kai-shek loses his cities and principal lines of communication to the Japanese and the countryside to the Communists.
>
> "The Communists have survived ten years of civil war and seven years of Japanese offensives. They have survived not only more sustained enemy pressure than the Chinese Central Government forces have been subjected to, but also a severe blockade imposed by Chiang.
>
> "They have survived and they have grown. . . . And they will continue to grow.
>
> "The reason for this phenomenal vitality and strength is simple and fundamental. It is mass support, mass participation. The Communist governments and armies are the first governments and armies in modern Chinese history to have positive and widespread popular support. They have this support because the governments and armies are genuinely of the people."[12]

These two excerpts from official reports to the Department of State express a point of view with respect to the situation in China which came to be ever more widely held

among Americans. But given this point of view as to Kuomintang deterioration, it would have been logical to have
withdrawn support from it or at least to have begun to establish direct relations with the Communists to the extent necessary to convince them that we were willing to treat them
not as members of a rebellious faction but as one of the two
major parties which should be drawn together to form the
government. This was proposed to the Department by the
American Chargé, George Atcheson, on February 26, 1945:

> "The initial step which we propose for con-
> sideration predicated on the assumption of the
> existence of the military necessity, is that the Presi-
> dent inform Chiang Kai-shek in definite terms that
> we are required by military necessity to cooperate
> with and supply the Communists and other suitable
> groups who can aid in this war against the Japan-
> ese, and that to accomplish this end, we are taking
> direct steps. Under existing conditions, this would
> not include forces which are not in actual position
> to attack the enemy, such as the Szechwan warlords.
> Chiang Kai-shek can be assured by us that we do
> not contemplate reduction of our assistance to the
> Central Government."[13]

These recommendations as to policy were "strongly opposed" by General Hurley, who had been recalled to Washington for consultations, "and it remained the policy of the
United States to supply military matériel and financial support only to the recognized Chinese National Government."[14]

(e) The Stilwell Period

An important consideration impelling the United States
to some sort of action was the situation in China as it affected
the war. The United States had assumed the primary role in

planning operations in the Pacific and Far East. In this planning, while considerable importance was attached to the China-Burma theater, the emphasis on it was partly negative. A substantial portion of Japan's military forces was contained in China as long as China's resistance was maintained. Consequently it was held essential to successful operations elsewhere that deterioration in China should not reach the point of causing the Chinese government to come to terms with Japan. This would have had even worse psychological than military effects since it was China's participation which prevented the Pacific war from assuming the appearance of a war of the East against the West, as Japanese propaganda sought to make it. To bolster Kuomintang China's morale and will to resist, consequently, it was necessary to hold out the prospect of sufficient material assistance not merely to enable the country to hold on but to give it the prospect of turning from the defensive to the offensive. For this purpose the mission headed by General Stilwell was sent to China:

> "(1) to supervise and control all United States defense-aid affairs for China; (2) under the Generalissimo to command all United States forces in China and such Chinese forces as may be assigned to him; (3) to represent the United States Government on any International War Council in China and act as the Chief of Staff for the Generalissimo; (4) to improve, maintain and control the Burma road in China."[15]

These functions assigned to General Stilwell in an allied country by his own government, whether designedly or not, reflected an adverse view as to the competence of that government. And the relationships which he established with the Generalissimo helped to sustain rather than to modify the view that the United States did not have confidence in the efficiency, the integrity, or the military judgment of the Chinese government.

> "The underlying basis of conflict between Stilwell and the Generalissimo," however, "was over the role which China should be prepared to play in the Pacific war. The former wanted to utilize American aid so as to bring China's total forces to bear on the Japanese in offensive land operations. To accomplish this, he came to the conclusion that it was necessary to undertake extensive retraining of the Chinese armies under American military leadership since he had little confidence in the military capabilities of the upper levels of the Chinese command. The attainment of the objective, as he saw it, further required: (1) that the national armies which were withdrawn from military operations against the Japanese to maintain the Kuomintang position against the Communists should be utilized against the Japanese, and (2) that the Communist armies should be similarly utilized and be supported for that purpose, and incorporated in his command."[16]

The low priority given to the China theater in Anglo-American strategic planning, indicated in the willingness to divert arms and other supplies allocated to the Chinese to meet what were viewed as more immediately pressing needs elsewhere, weakened the force of Stilwell's argument without changing the growing tendency in the United States to think of China as not concentrating her full efforts on the Japanese war and to become increasingly critical of the government and the Generalissimo for that reason.[17] The available evidence seems to indicate that the Generalissimo had reached the conclusion, which all of the military planning and actions seemed to confirm, that the war was to be won in any case without the use of China as a primary base for an offensive. Thus he was not impelled to put war operations ahead of considerations of domestic politics. This meant that he was unwilling voluntarily to weaken his position against the Communists "either by withdrawal of his own troops for use against the Japanese, except in an extreme emergency, or to permit operations by the Communist armies throughout China, even if it had been possible to bring them under American command"[18] without any weakening of his own authority.

The circumstances of the war had already resulted in an enlargement through guerrilla operations of the area of Communist influence and a contraction of the Kuomintang area. With an eye to control of the situation after the war, the policy evolved was that of "containment" of the Communists within their area. Military dispositions were made with this in mind. This was justified on the ground that the Communists were themselves conducting a war within a war, not having honestly subordinated themselves to either the political or the military authority of the national government.[19] The Stilwell policy, however, could only have disturbed the existing status, and, as viewed by the Kuomintang, to the advantage of the Communists.

In searching for arguments designed to lessen American pressure for acceptance of the Stilwell proposals (which represented the policy of the War Department), the Generalissimo raised the issue of Russian-Chinese Communist relations, taking the position, in conversations with Vice President Wallace, that in spite of Communist propaganda to the effect that they were not tied to the U.S.S.R. and "were in effect nothing more than agrarian democrats," in fact the Chinese Communists "follow the orders of the Third In-

ternational." When Mr. Wallace "mentioned the fact that
the Third International had been dissolved . . . President
Chiang indicated that the situation had not been altered by
that fact."[20]

The question of the nature of the Chinese Communist
Party and of its relation to the U.S.S.R. came to be a consideration in the development of American China policy before the end of the war. With this was joined the question
of Soviet policy toward China itself. American policy was
based initially on the view that the Chinese Communist Party
was a party of agrarian reform, willing to participate in government within a democratic framework, and without foreign
governmental support. This view of the nature of the Chinese
Communist Party was, as Chiang Kai-shek pointed out, one
disseminated by the Party itself. It was, however, confirmed
by the observations of those Americans who had access as
reporters to the Communist area and who saw an apparent
policy of agrarian reform being applied and a form of democratic participation in local government in operation. But
General Hurley initially carried it authoritatively to China
as a support for the policy which he followed.

(f) The Hurley Policy

When General Patrick J. Hurley was appointed Personal
Representative of President Roosevelt to China on August
18, 1944, it was with a view to the adjustment of relations
between General Stilwell and Chiang Kai-shek and in anticipation that such adjustment would result in the implementation of the Stilwell policy. This is indicated in President
Roosevelt's communication of August 23.

"I am glad that you [the Generalissimo] find
General Hurley and Mr. Nelson acceptable for the
important mission they will perform for us. Now

that my personal representatives to you have been decided upon, I think we should proceed immediately to take the positive steps demanded by the military situation. I urge that you take the necessary measures to place General Stilwell in command of the Chinese forces, under your direction, at the earliest possible date. . . . I feel certain, however, that between General Hurley and General Stilwell there will be an adequate comprehension of the political problems you face. I am urging action in the matter of Stilwell's appointment so strongly because I feel that, with further delay, it may be too late to avert a military catastrophe tragic both to China and to our allied plans for the early overthrow of Japan. . . . I do not think the forces to come under General Stilwell's command should be limited except by their availability to defend China and fight the Japanese. . . ."[21]

General Hurley, of course, failed to make an adjustment, on the terms sought by the President and the War Department, between General Stilwell and the Generalissimo. The recall of General Stilwell from China, at the demand of Chiang Kai-shek, was announced on October 24, 1944. His political functions were absorbed by the Personal Representative of the President, as were finally those of the Ambassador, the duties of which office General Hurley took over with the presentation of his credentials as American Ambassador on January 8, 1945.

It is evident that General Hurley took a broad view of the purposes of his mission, since he went to Moscow en route to Chungking to ascertain Soviet views concerning the China problem. In the course of his conversation with the Soviet Foreign Minister, General Hurley was informed that:

"Although he [Molotov] said that the Soviet government had unjustifiably been held responsible for various happenings in China during recent years, Molotov stressed that it would bear no responsibility for internal affairs or developments in China. Molotov then spoke of the very impoverished conditions of the people in parts of China, some of whom called themselves Communists but were related to Communism in no way at all. It was merely a way of expressing dissatisfaction with their economic condition and that they would forget this political inclination when their economic condition improved. The Soviet government should not be associated with these 'communist elements' nor could it in any way be blamed for this situation. . . . Molotov's satisfaction at being consulted was clearly indicated. He gave little new information but he confirmed statements made previously that his government would be glad to see the United States taking the lead economically, politically, and militarily in Chinese affairs."[22]

On the basis of this expression of opinion General Hurley felt that he could reassure the Generalissimo and persuade him that it was safe for him to negotiate a new agreement with the Chinese Communists. Reporting in December 1944, he noted:

"At the time I came here Chiang Kai-shek believed that the Communist Party in China was an instrument of the Soviet Government in Russia. He is now convinced that the Russian Government does not recognize the Chinese Communist Party as Communist at all and that (1) Russia is not supporting the Communist Party in China, (2)

Russia does not want dissensions or civil war in China, and (3) Russia desires more harmonious relations with China.

". . . He now feels that he can reach a settlement with the Communist Party as a Chinese political party without foreign entanglements."[23]

Events soon revealed, however, that the Chinese Communist Party, without Soviet support, felt strong enough to set its own conditions for unity, and that the Generalissimo was sufficiently distrustful of its strength and its intentions not to accept what General Hurley felt was "a practical plan for settlement with the Communists." This plan involved the reorganization of the existing National Government "into a coalition National government embracing representatives of all anti-Japanese parties and non-partisan political bodies. A new democratic policy providing for reform in military, political, economic and cultural affairs shall be promulgated and made effective. At the same time the National Military Council is to be reorganized into the United National Council consisting of representatives of all anti-Japanese armies." It was further stipulated that the "coalition National Government of China recognizes the legality of the Kuomintang of China, the Chinese Communist Party and all anti-Japanese parties."[24] Thus the Communists proposed unity on the basis of an agreed termination of the Kuomintang one-party system of government through the institution of a government formed by a coalition of parties. To this government, not that of the Generalissimo, they proposed to transfer direction but not necessarily control of all armies, including their own. And in this connection they stipulated that "the supplies acquired from foreign powers will be equitably distributed." This stipulation could mean only their understanding that their armies would retain their separate organization and would begin to get a *pro rata* allotment of matériel from abroad.

During the entire period of subsequent negotiations, the Communist position remained that of advocacy of the formation of a coalition government in advance of the amalgamation of military forces into a national army. Since what they proposed seemed to the Americans involved to be a move toward the establishment of unity on a democratic basis, the Communist position seemed to be more consistent with American policy objectives than was the apparent unwillingness of the Generalissimo immediately to modify the Kuomintang monopoly of legality and power so as to include the Communists. Coalition as understood by the Americans meant participation of all organized political groups in a common government and in the formation of public policy by adjustment of various points of view to one another through discussion. Thus coalition was thought of as a movement toward the establishment in good faith of a democratic system in place of the imposed rule of one party. It was not then understood to be a tactical maneuver designed to enable the dictatorship of one party ultimately to be replaced by the dictatorship of the other.

The Kuomintang view, however, as expressed in conferences at the beginning of 1945, was "that the real purpose of the Chinese Communist Party was not the abolition of the one-party rule by the Kuomintang but rather, as indicated by all the maneuvers made by the Chinese Communists, to overthrow control by the Kuomintang Party and obtain a one-party rule of China by the Chinese Communist Party."[25] Consequently the Central Government refused to accept the draft proposals which General Hurley brought back from Yenan. As an alternative to the Communist "Five-Point Plan" it formulated a Three-Point counter-proposal as a basis for cooperation:

"(1) The National Government, desirous of securing effective unification and concentration of all military forces in China for the purpose of accomplishing the speedy defeat of Japan, and looking forward to the post-war reconstruction of China, agrees to incorporate, after reorganization, the Chinese Communist forces in the National Army who will then receive equal treatment as the other units in respect to pay, allowance, munitions and other supplies, and to give recognition to the Chinese Communist Party as a legal party.

"(2) The Communist Party undertakes to give their full support to the National Government in the prosecution of the war of resistance, and in the post-war reconstruction, and give over control of all their troops to the National Government through the National Military Council. The National Government will designate some high ranking officers from among the Communist forces to membership in the National Military Council.

"(3) The aim of the National Government to which the Communist Party subscribes is to carry out the Three People's Principles of Dr. Sun Yat-sen for the establishment in China of a government of the people, for the people and by the people and it will pursue policies designed to promote the progress and development of democratic processes in government.

"In accordance with the provisions of the *Program of Armed Resistance and National Reconstruction,* freedom of speech, freedom of the press, freedom of assembly and association and other civil liberties are hereby guaranteed, subject only to the

specific needs of security in the effective prosecution
of the war against Japan."[26]

This proposal was in essence that the Communists should
give up their power position and resume their allegiance to
the government in exchange for the promise of legality for
the Party, the participation in military direction of such of
their leaders as were designated by Chiang Kai-shek, and
the guarantee of civil liberties. If it had been accepted and
put into effect it would have lessened the possibility of civil
war and removed the principal excuse for the failure of the
Kuomintang to end the period of tutelage and devote its
energies to economic reform and reconstruction after the end
of the war. But its acceptance would have made the Communists completely dependent upon the good faith of the
Kuomintang in the fulfillment of its promises, including
those essential to its successful functioning as a legal political
party. They did not have sufficient confidence in the Kuomintang to dispose them to give up their independent military
power except to a government in which they effectively participated.

If the United States had had a greater confidence in the
National Government, and if it had been willing to act
unequivocally and decisively in support of the policy of that
Government against the Communists, the situation after the
Japanese surrender might still have developed into civil
war but the outcome might have been quite different. A clear
declaration of intention to support the recognized government, even by military means, would probably have involved
the United States as a participant in the civil war since there
is no reason to believe that the Communists would have
accepted Chiang Kai-shek's terms at the demand of the
United States. If they had not it would have been difficult to
prevent the immediate outbreak of civil war even before the

end of the Japanese war. If not then, the situation at the time of Japanese surrender would have involved operations against the Communists while taking over the territories occupied by the Japanese.

Consequently the Hurley policy, and subsequently that of General Marshall, while based upon support of the government, was directed toward the negotiation of a settlement which would prevent the outbreak of civil war by bringing the Communists into the government. The idea of negotiation, it must be repeated, required that the Communists be viewed as entitled to consideration of their views as far as possible on an equality with the government. This was difficult to the extent to which the United States was actually in a position of lending assistance to the government but not to the Communists. The inevitable result was that the United States came to be viewed by the Communists as intervening in China's domestic affairs, but without the good will of the non-Communists or the anti-Communists being secured.

(g) The Problem of Implementing the Surrender Terms

The end of the Japanese war found the Kuomintang and the Communists in the same relative position with respect to one another as at the beginning of 1945. The Hurley-sponsored negotiations had produced no agreement, but the Generalissimo's government had not collapsed, in spite of a successful Japanese offensive in China, and the Communist position was still undisturbed. Aside from these unresolved internal differences and difficulties, the problem of internal relationship was complicated by the requirement that the occupied area be taken over and the Japanese troops repatriated.

From the standpoint of the United States, VJ Day did not end its responsibilities in the China theater. These, it was held, continued until China was completely free from Japanese military control. Consequently the United States felt an obligation to offer the necessary assistance to the government of China to enable its troops and officials to move back into the provinces from which the Japanese had driven the National Government after 1931. Since Chiang Kai-shek had been designated to receive the Japanese surrender in China, authorization had to be secured from him to act in behalf of China. He refused such authorization to the Communists even with respect to the areas adjacent to theirs within which they had established local governments during the course of the war. But the National Government did not have transport facilities of its own to enable it to move its own troops and officials rapidly into North China. Consequently the American government put the necessary facilities at its disposal.

"In order to assist the Government in reoccupying Japanese-held areas and opening lines of communication, the United States immediately after V-J Day transported three Nationalist armies by air to key sectors of East and North China, including Shanghai, Nanking and Peiping, and likewise during the ensuing months provided water transport for an additional large number of troops until, according to Department of the Army figures, between 400,000 and 500,000 Chinese soldiers had been moved to new positions. . . . In order to assist the government further in maintaining control of certain key areas of North China and in repatriating the Japanese, and at the request of the National Government, over 50,000 United States Marines were landed in North China and occupied Peiping, Tientsin, and the coal mines to the north, together with the essential railroads in the area.

With such American assistance, forces of the Generalissimo, who had been designated by SCAP as the sole agent to receive the surrender of Japanese forces in China proper, were able to effect the surrender of the great majority of the 1,200,000 Japanese troops stationed there, together with their equipment and stocks of military matériel."[27]

While this American assistance to the National Government was viewed by the United States as in continuation of the common war effort and as directed toward anti-Japanese war objectives, and while any intention to intervene in China's domestic politics was disclaimed,[28] the fact remains that it had the effect of enabling the National Government to win the race against the Communists for control of those North and East China areas which the Japanese had occupied. This brought Chiang's troops into a new position of contact and conflict with the Communist armies since the latter continued to control the North China countryside as they had during the Japanese occupation. The result was that the

"American military authorities and their occupation forces were placed in the unsatisfactory position of finding themselves in between the two contending factions. Civil war broke out. It was attended by loud outcries within the United States from those who sympathized with the Communist faction, demanding the immediate withdrawal of every American soldier from China. It was met with equal virulence on the part of those who sympathized with the National Government, and who believed that Moscow was utilizing the Chinese Communist armies to establish its own immediate control over China and thereby to overthrow the National Government."[29]

This pressure, together with its inherited tendency against military intervention in China to implement its policies and insistence that it was aiding China against Japan and not supporting one faction against another, led the United States quickly to withdraw most of its troops from China. However, the United States continued to give non-military aid to China exclusively through the medium of the National Government. Military assistance was maintained by the continuation of a relatively modest military training program, and by the sale or loan of surplus military supplies.

"The aid (totalling by 1949 in all categories approximately two billion dollars) was sufficient to commit the United States to the National Government, and thus to arouse continued hostility on the part of the Communists and of other opponents of the Kuomintang regime. It was, however, insufficient so to strengthen the National Government as to enable it to maintain itself in North China and Manchuria against the Communists. In effect, the lessening of American support of the Kuomintang government constituted negatively an intervention in favor of the Communists since the measure of superiority of the government forces was the extent of American aid.[30] Whatever course it took after 1945, in other words, the United States was liable to be accused of intervention in China's civil war."[31]

It was under these circumstances that President Truman defined American postwar policy toward China on December 15, 1945. Aside from a justification along lines indicated above, of American assistance to the National Government in the take-over from the Japanese, the President defined American policy as follows:

"It is the firm belief of this Government that a strong, united and democratic China is of the utmost importance to the success of the United Nations organization and for world peace. A China disorganized and divided either by foreign aggression, such as that undertaken by the Japanese, or by violent internal strife, is an undermining influence to world stability and peace, now and in the future. The United States Government has long subscribed to the principle that the management of internal affairs is the responsibility of the peoples of the sovereign nations. Events of this century, however, would indicate that a breach of peace anywhere in the world threatens the peace of the entire world. It is thus in the most vital interest of the United States and all the United Nations that the people of China overlook no opportunity to adjust their internal differences promptly by means of peaceful negotiation.

"The Government of the United States believes it essential:

"(1) That a cessation of hostilities be arranged between the armies of the National Government and the Chinese Communists and other dissident Chinese armed forces for the purpose of completing the return of all China to effective Chinese control, including the immediate evacuation of the Japanese forces.

"(2) That a national conference of representatives of major political elements be arranged to develop an early solution to the present internal strife—a solution which will bring about the unification of China.

"The United States and the other United Nations have recognized the present National Government of the Republic of China as the only legal government in China. It is the proper instrument to achieve the objective of a unified China. . . .

"The United States is cognizant that the present National Government of China is a 'one-party government' and believes that peace, unity and democratic reform in China will be furthered if the basis of this Government is broadened to include other political elements in the country. Hence the United States strongly advocates that the national conference of representatives of major political elements in the country agree upon arrangements which would give those elements a fair and effective representation in the Chinese National Government. It is recognized that this would require modification of the one-party 'political tutelage' established as an interim arrangement in the progress of the nation toward political democracy by the father of the Chinese Republic, Doctor Sun Yat-sen.

"The existence of autonomous armies such as that of the Communist army is inconsistent with, and actually makes impossible, political unity in China. With the institution of a broadly representative government, autonomous armies should be eliminated as such and all armed forces in China integrated effectively into the Chinese National Army."[32]

Beyond this, the President declared the willingness of the United States to assist financially and otherwise in the economic, political, and military rehabilitation and reconstruction of the country "as China moves toward peace and unity along the lines described above."

(h) Application of American Policy by General Marshall

This policy, which General Marshall was sent to China to implement, did not represent a new departure but it did involve an important shift in emphasis. Although the intention to continue recognition of the National Government and to work with and through it was reaffirmed, the emphasis was put on reform and reconstruction rather than on preventing the collapse of the National Government and sustaining the Generalissimo (except insofar as reform was viewed as having that consequence). A second shift was from the view that political participation in the National Government should be the inducement to the Communists to bring their armies under National Government control, to the view that representation of all groups should be provided and that "with the institution of a broadly representative government," then "autonomous armies should be eliminated as such. . . ." The perception that there were the two elements in the problem, however, continued to exist.

In spite of this second shift in emphasis, the situation in North China when General Marshall arrived put the military side of the problem first. Since the primary American objective was to prevent the outbreak of civil war so that a settlement could be negotiated, the first requirement was necessarily felt to be agreement to stop the actual fighting. In anticipation of General Marshall's arrival the National Government had moved toward realization of the American government's political objective by constituting the People's Consultative Conference.

> "The P.C.C. lasted for 22 days. Its most important act was the freezing of military positions by the Agreement of January 10, 1946, whereby a Committee of Three (Kuomintang, Communist, American) undertook the stopping of the civil war.

Troops on both sides were to maintain positions. The Communists promised not to interfere with lines of communication and explicitly admitted the government's right to fulfill its international obligation by reoccupying Manchuria after fifteen years of Japanese invasion."[33]

The convocation of the People's Consultative Conference indicated the Kuomintang Government's determination to maintain its position as "the proper instrument to achieve the objective of a unified China" and to set and control the conditions for the termination of the period of "one-party tutelage." It adhered to this position of initiative throughout, itself setting the conditions of reform and finally formally ending the period of tutelage with the adoption of the constitution, promulgated January 1, 1947, to become effective December 25, 1947.

The Communists had participated in the P.C.C. and had accepted the Truce Agreement, however, with the understanding that the next steps would be the legalization of parties, and the broadening of the base of the government through coalition so that they would be effective participants in working out a satisfactory permanent framework of government. In other words they were not prepared to accept the Kuomintang Government as the proper instrument to achieve unification through political reorganization and reconstruction. Consequently they were not willing to give up their autonomous armies which were the instruments of their power, until they felt secure in their ability to maintain themselves by political means.

The Truce Agreement obviously did not affect the fundamental elements of the problem. If it had been fully implemented in good faith by both sides, as was not the case, it might have stabilized conditions sufficiently so as to have enabled General Marshall to play his mediatory role more successfully. In this respect it was an essential preliminary to an attempt to solve the underlying problem, but it was not actually a part of that solution, except as it helped to break down the suspicion which each side had of the good faith of the other. As General Marshall stated, January 7, 1947, in estimating the reasons for his failure to secure agreement between the two sides:

"In the first place, the greatest obstacle to peace has been the complete, almost overwhelming suspicion with which the Chinese Communist Party and the Kuomintang regard each other.

"On the one hand, the leaders of the Government are strongly opposed to a communistic form of government. On the other, the Communists state frankly that they are Marxists and intend to work toward establishing a communistic form of government in China, though first advancing through the medium of a democratic form of government of the American or British type.

"The leaders of the Government are convinced in their minds that the Communist-expressed desire to participate in a government of the type endorsed by the Political Consultative Conference last January had for its purpose only a destructive intention. The Communists felt, I believe, that the Government was insincere in its apparent acceptance of the PCC resolution for the formation of the new government and intended by coercion of military force and the action of secret police to obliterate the Communist Party."[34]

The truce itself, as far as it was actually enforced, proved to have been of advantage to the Communists rather than the

Kuomintang when full scale civil war broke out in the last half of 1947, following recognition of the failure of American mediation efforts. When the truce began the National Government armies had the initiative and were on the offensive. The activity of the truce teams in applying the terms of the agreement prevented the Nationalist armies from attaining their objectives and from wiping out large bodies of Communist troops. The period of the truce gave the Communists the necessary time to recover, and in their turn to assume the offensive. This, of course, was not a planned result of American policy, since it was assumed that the stabilization of the military positions of the Kuomintang and the Communists would enable the conditions of permanent peace to be negotiated. Nor was it only the time factor which enabled the Communists in North China to assume the offensive and to retain the initiative. Of even greater importance was the development of the situation in Manchuria and the effects of developments there on the struggle for power in China.

(i) The Soviet Union in Manchuria and United States Policy

To relate these developments to the situation in China it is necessary to go back to the war and to another aspect of American policy. Believing that a Japanese surrender could be secured only by invasion, it was the policy of the American government to induce the Soviet Union to enter the war against Japan. At the Teheran Conference Stalin had declared this to be the intention of his government when Germany had been finally defeated. As the end of the European war approached, however, qualifications began to be made to this declaration of intention. By the time of the Yalta Conference it was apparently necessary either to forgo Russian action against Japan or to promise the Soviet Union sufficient compensation to ensure its participation. The promised compensation was mainly at the expense of China rather than Japan since with the exception of the Yalta promise to recognize the *status quo* in Outer Mongolia and to hand over the Kuriles, it was agreed that Russian rights gained from China, but transferred from Russia to Japan as a result of Japanese use of force in and after 1904, should be reestablished. It was agreed that, while China should "retain full sovereignty in Manchuria" Russian rights would be restored much as they had existed at the time of outbreak of the Russo-Japanese war of 1904-1905. China did not participate in the negotiation of the Yalta Agreements, but the Americans and British pledged themselves to the fulfillment of their terms, and President Roosevelt undertook to secure their acceptance by Chiang Kai-shek.

This acceptance was embodied in the Sino-Soviet treaty of 1945. The major advantage of this treaty to the National Government was that it reestablished friendly relations and an alliance against Japan between the Soviet Union and China exclusively through the medium of the National Government. Article Five reads: "The High Contracting Parties, having regard to the interests of the security and economic development of each of them, agree to work together in close and friendly collaboration after the coming of peace and to act according to the principles of mutual respect for their sovereignty and territorial integrity and of non-interference in the internal affairs of the other contracting party." This is carried further in Article Six: "The High Contracting Parties agree to render each other every possible economic assistance in the post-war period with a view to facilitating and accelerating reconstruction in both countries and to contributing to the cause of world prosperity." And in a supplementary exchange of notes Molotov went the final step when he wrote: ". . . The Government of the U.S.S.R. agrees to render to China moral support and aid in military supplies and other material resources, such support and aid to be entirely given to the National Government as the central government of China."[35]

Russia declared war on Japan on August 8, 1945. The Surrender Instruments were signed on September 2 but acceptance of the surrender terms came on August 15. Consequently there was only a week during which real resistance to Russian arms was made by the Japanese Kwantung Army, but three weeks for the Soviet armies to establish themselves throughout Manchuria. The immediate effect of Soviet occupancy of Manchuria was to strip it of much of its industrial plant, which was removed as "war booty" to Russian territory. It was also made virtually a closed territory so far as Russia's allies were concerned. The removals made it more difficult to deal with the question of Japanese reparations, and, of greater importance, ensured that the territory, if and when restored to China's control, would not immediately have the industrial importance which Chinese planning had attached to it in relation to the economic reconstruction of China itself.

At Yalta, President Roosevelt had acquiesced in Russia's postwar reentry into Manchuria under military advice that that was not too great a price to pay for a Soviet declaration of war against Japan. But, with this restoration of the status of about 1899, American policy assumed substantially the form given it by Secretary John Hay. This was to protest any expansion of rights beyond those formally conceded and to seek to protect American interests within the new legal framework. Thus Secretary Byrnes, on February 9, 1946, instructed the American embassies to express the following views to the Chinese and Soviet governments:

"The Sino-Soviet Treaty and agreements signed August 14, 1945, provide for joint Sino-Soviet

control over certain trunk railways in Manchuria,
but these agreements exclude reference to any similar control over industrial enterprise in Manchuria.
It is the understanding of the United States Government, which was kept informed of the course
of negotiations which led up to the agreements,
that exclusive Sino-Soviet governmental control
over Manchurian enterprise would be limited to the
railways dealt with in the aforesaid agreements. It
is therefore disturbing to this Government to receive reports that discussions are under way which
might result in the establishment of exclusive Sino-
Soviet control over industrial enterprises in Manchuria. Under present conditions, when free access
to Manchuria is not open to nationals of other
powers and equality of opportunity in seeking participation in the economic development of Manchuria is denied Americans and other Allied nationals, it is felt that negotiation of agreements
between the Chinese and Russian governments
with regard to industries in Manchuria would be
contrary to the principle of the Open Door, would
constitute clear discrimination against Americans
who might wish an opportunity to participate in
the development of Manchurian industry and
might place American commercial interests at a distinct disadvantage in establishing future trade relations with Manchuria."[36]

In the same communication the Secretary of State related
the question to that of reparations policy for Japan. "Directly related to this matter of the industries in Manchuria
is the matter of reparations policy for Japan because the
major portion of the industries of Manchuria were Japanese-

owned prior to the defeat of Japan. This Government considers that the ultimate disposition of Japanese external assets, such as the industries in Manchuria, is a matter of common interest and concern to those Allies who bore the major burden in defeating Japan. . . ." And the same general point of view as that expressed with respect to industry was advanced with respect to the consolidation and expansion of Russian rights at Dairen. Such issues were, however, to be negotiated. An attempt to enforce American policy in Manchuria was not indicated then or subsequently, nor did developing circumstances give any reason to believe that it could be implemented. Those circumstances again made Manchuria a part of the larger problem presented by China itself.

Russia did not directly violate Molotov's pledge to assist in the postwar reconstruction of China exclusively through the medium of the National Government. But the stripping of Manchuria of its plant capacity, even though Japanese-owned, was not the action of a friend. And the conditions of transfer of Manchuria to Chinese control were certainly an indirect but effective method of assisting the unrecognized Communists against the recognized National Government. In literal fulfillment of their commitments to the National Government, the Soviet authorities refused to admit Communist armed forces as such into Manchuria. Unarmed "civilians" were admitted in large numbers, however, and were permitted to arm themselves from the armament taken from the Japanese. Consequently, when the Kuomintang forces arrived they were faced by organized and equipped Communist forces. The National Government forces were permitted only very restricted entry through the Russian-controlled ports, so that they had to enter by land routes which the Communists attempted to block. Consequently, extensive military operations had to be undertaken if Manchuria was to be brought under control by the National Government. These operations, undertaken against the advice of the American Military Mission, were considered by Chiang Kai-shek as necessitated by the exigencies of domestic politics. They proved ultimately disastrous to the position of the National Government since they stretched its limited military resources too far. The troops sent to Manchuria were lost because of inability to keep them supplied and reenforced. Thus the disparity between the Communists and the National Government in China itself was lessened by the one-sided losses in Manchuria.

> "As the struggle for Manchuria continued, the Communists found arms and equipment replacements available from northern Manchuria and Siberia where the Russians had brought back into use some of the looted arsenal plant facilities. A further source of supply was in the American equipment acquired through the surrender of government troops. From Manchuria, as they solidified their position, they were also able to supply the Communist armies of North China so that the original superiority in arms of the Kuomintang forces, which compelled the Communists to continue their wartime guerrilla tactics, and kept the major cities out of reach of their forces, was replaced by Communist superiority."[37]

From the military standpoint this superiority was clearly manifest by 1949. Military superiority was, however, partly the result of increasing loss of morale within the National Government and the Kuomintang, paralleling constantly deteriorating economic conditions and lessening of confidence in the integrity and efficiency of the national leadership. Recurrent American expressions of lack of confidence in the honesty and efficiency of the National Government helped to strengthen this view in China as well as in the United States, and were an important factor in weakening the government in its struggle against the Communists. Thus, although it was American policy to support the National Government, the methods of expression of policy actually served to weaken it.

By 1949, China north of the Yangtze was under Communist military control. The National Government then sought to settle by negotiation. To make this possible Chiang Kai-shek went on leave of absence from the presidential office, leaving to Li Tsung-jen, the Vice-President, who took over administration of the powers of the President, the responsibility of coming to terms with the Communists. Since their terms proved to be, in effect, unconditional surrender, so far as the Kuomintang and its leaders were concerned, the war was resumed. By the end of October the Communist armies had occupied Canton, having previously driven the National Government forces from Nanking, Shanghai, and Hankow. The government then established itself in Formosa and Hainan, the western portion of China having also been brought under Communist control. Hainan later fell to the Communists, in the spring of 1950, leaving the Nationalists restricted to a precarious hold on the island of Formosa off the Fukien coast.

This outcome posed a new problem for the United States Government. This was whether or not to acquiesce formally in the new situation by according recognition to the government which the Communists had organized and proclaimed for the new "People's Republic of China" on September 21, 1949. It was recognized by the Soviet Union on October 2, and thereafter by other governments which were accustomed to follow Soviet policy in international affairs, and by Britain and some other states.

(j) The United States Policy of Non-Recognition

The United States government had followed a policy of non-recognition of the new regime. One of the reasons given was Peiping's unwillingness to enter into relations on the basis of observance of the accepted amenities of international practice. The evidence, so far as the United States was concerned, was altogether to the contrary, as indicated in the treatment accorded American diplomatic and consular representatives when the Communists took over, and in the declared intention of the Communists not to be bound by any engagements made by China during the Kuomintang period. Another factor in establishing officially the policy of non-recognition was the possibility of impermanence in the Communist regime. Resistance to it was maintained by Chiang Kai-shek from Formosa and it was not altogether clear that it had effectively established its authority over China, since there were some evidences of growing hostility to it, and its head, Mao Tse-tung, referred to the problem of disposing of the opposition of some three to four hundred thousand "bandits," who might be guerrillas. Finally, the growing support within the United States of action designed to "contain" Communism made it necessary for the government to move carefully, if it moved at all toward recognition of the Peiping regime.

Another area of policy which was affected by the changed situation in China and by the question of recognition was in the United Nations. There the Chinese (National Government) delegations not only continued to represent China but they also formally preferred charges against the Soviet Union of having been instrumental in bringing about the change in China. This led the Soviet Government to withdraw from participation in any United Nations organ in which the National Government representatives were allowed a seat. It demanded the seating of representatives for China of the government which it had recognized, since it held that this alone conformed to the realities of the situation.

The United States supported the National Government within the United Nations, both in its demand for a hearing on its charges against the Soviet Union and in its right to continue to hold China's seat. Secretary of State Acheson, however, took the position that the United States would not exercise its right of veto on the question in the Security Council but would accept the decision of the requisite majority there, in the General Assembly at its next meeting, and in other organs of the United Nations. This continued the policy of non-use of the veto on all but enforcement or substantive issues. Later, Secretary Acheson qualified this approach, in the course of his testimony before the Senate inquiry into the dismissal of General MacArthur. Should the United States find itself in a minority on the Security Council in its opposition to seating the Chinese Communists, he said, it would appeal to the International Court of Justice to rule whether the power of veto was applicable. But it was clearly anticipated or hoped that the United States would have sufficient influence to prevent the necessary majority vote for seating the Communists in place of the National Government representatives, and up to July 1951 a majority favored the American position.

The absence of the Soviet representatives, of course, prevented the normal functioning of United Nations organs. But this absence made it impossible for the Soviet Union to exercise a positive veto when the United States took the question of the invasion of the Korean Republic by the Communist Northern Korean forces on June 25, 1950 to the Security Council.

4. United States Korean Policy

Korea had been a bone of contention between Japan and Russia from the enforced recognition of its independence of China in 1895 until its annexation by Japan after the Russo-Japanese war of 1904-1905. Under Japanese domination, independence agitation was ruthlessly suppressed so that by the outbreak of World War II those who advocated it had to do so in exile or by underground terroristic methods in Korea. The earliest group of exiles, following the suppression of the demand for independence and self-determination in 1919, established themselves in the United States. By 1945, however, there had been established a center at Chungking in China, organized into a provisional government. But by that time probably the largest number of revolutionary "overseas" Koreans had found harborage in the Russian Far East.

From the standpoint of American policy, Korean independence had been recognized in the treaty of 1876, but the United States had acquiesced in the successive changes made thereafter in the country's status. The Cairo Declaration of December 1, 1943, however, affirmed as war policy the intention to bring Japan back within its territorial limits of 1894. This required the establishment of policy with respect to Korea as well as Manchuria and Formosa. It was then declared that Formosa would be restored to China. Korea, on the other hand, was to become free and independent, but "in due course," rather than immediately at the end of the war.

The qualification seems to have been made because of the

57

belief that the relatively long period of subjugation, during which Koreans had been denied participation in government and during which they had been more and more completely assimilated into the Japanese structure economically as well as politically, had left them unprepared to assume immediately the responsibilities of self-government. The possibility of bringing Koreans in the United States and in China together so as to form a "government-in-exile" to be developed to the point where a trained and somewhat experienced Korean democratic leadership could go into Korea with the Allied armies to take over, with allied assistance, from the Japanese, was only beginning to be seriously developed by VJ Day. One reason for the American-British-Chinese failure to proceed along this line was doubt as to the ability of those who had been living long in exile to translate their leadership of "overseas" Koreans into leadership within Korea. It was not known whether, or to what extent, an internal leadership existed within Korea which might have to be reckoned with as a force competitive with that of the exiles. These doubts concerning the development of a native government apparently did not enter as much into Soviet calculations as they did into those of the United States.

> "With Soviet participation in the war, four rather than the original three Powers [China, the United States, Britain] had an interest in the future of Korea, in addition to the Koreans themselves. But by the time of Japanese surrender the immediately effective voices had been reduced to those of the United States and the Soviet Union. They seemed then to be prepared initially to put into effect a civilian four-power 'trustee' supervision of the governments of an otherwise independent Korea for the limited period necessary to bring about an

orderly creation of a new government to which complete responsibility could be transferred."[38]

To facilitate the rapid military take-over from the Japanese and the repatriation of Japanese troops and civilians, however, it was agreed "that Japanese troops north of the 38th parallel should surrender to Soviet forces and that those south of the 38th parallel should surrender to United States forces."[39] This proved to be one of those decisions, justified in military terms, which had as important political as military consequences since it divided Korea into two zones and made it impossible for Korean independence to be established except on the basis of United States-Soviet agreement. This proved to be impossible, as neither party was willing to acquiesce in any solution which could be viewed as having the effect of strengthening the position of the other.

The local commands could not agree on the conditions of local interzonal intercourse during 1945. The broader question, when taken up at the December 1945 Moscow Conference of Foreign Ministers, was solved by agreement in principle on the establishment of a provisional Korean democratic government for the entire country. This government was to be set up by a Joint Commission, itself to be created on the basis of recommendations made to the Four Powers by the United States and Soviet Commands in Korea "in consultation with Korean democratic parties and social organizations." The Joint Commission and the Provisional Government, when established, were then to propose for consideration the terms of a Four-Power five-year trusteeship agreement.

The idea of international trusteeship and thus the postponement of independence was rejected by all shades of Korean opinion except the Communist. Since the Soviet Government took the position that no groups should be consulted which had not "shown a willingness to accept fully and freely" the Moscow decisions, which eliminated all but the Communists, and since the American government refused to consider consultation except on a broad democratic basis, the Joint Commission, established in March 1946, was unable to proceed. This impasse continued into 1947 and finally the United States took the question of Korean independence to the United Nations, at the second regular session of the General Assembly. Possibly to avoid Assembly intervention along lines acceptable to the United States, or possibly because of confidence in an outcome within Korea acceptable to itself, the Soviet Government at that time proposed the simultaneous withdrawal of the military forces of the occupying powers, thus letting the Koreans organize their own government without outside assistance. This proposal was not acceptable to the United States, which apparently felt that such action would lead to an extension of Communist and thus Soviet control over the southern zone from the northern. The proposal was also rejected by the General Assembly.

The basis for this American view was the knowledge that the Soviet authorities had organized their zone rapidly and effectively under a Korean Communist Party. "On February 9, 1946, a Provisional People's Committee for North Korea was established as the central governing organ, and the various political parties . . . were united in a single new People's Party. An all-Korean 'cabinet' was formed, headed by Kim Il-sung, a famous Korean revolutionist and Communist."[40] Controlled elections were held in November 1946, which resulted "in a sweeping endorsement of candidates chosen by the single party."[41] Under the auspices of this government, furthermore, immediate steps were taken to establish a North Korean army. Consequently, by September 1947, when the Americans took the issue to the United Nations, the Russians had brought into being a mechanism of government and a military force which they had every reason to believe would continue to accept their direction despite a withdrawal of their military forces.

During this period the major efforts of the United States had been directed toward agreement on the conditions of unification of the two zones. At the same time, to be sure, it had faced the problem of government in South Korea, but had attempted its solution quite differently. In the first place, instead of picking out a Korean group or groups through which to work from the beginning, the United States worked through Japanese rather than Korean administrators, although under American direction, during the first months of liberation. This did not present to the Koreans the appearance of liberation. Then authority was transferred, in January 1946, to the United States Military Government regime, under which Koreans were progressively given administrative but not political responsibility during 1946. An Advisory Council, made up of essentially conservative Koreans, was, however, constituted in February 1946. "It was replaced in November by an Interim Legislative Assembly half of whose members were selected by a system of indirect elections, the other half being appointed by the Military Government."[42] There was much opposition to the election plans, which showed itself in "strikes, riots, and open rebellion. . . . Leftist elements accused the military government of suppressing all but conservative activity in a reign of terror, while the American command announced that the agitation was a communist plot. A sweeping conservative victory took place at the polls in the midst of this confusion, but even the middle-of-the-road Korean leaders declared the elections to have been fraudulent."[43]

Some of the mistakes made by the United States, which slowed up the effective political organization of its zone, were undoubtedly due to ignorance of Korean conditions and attitudes. Unquestionably, also, some of them were due to a desire to establish a democratic regime, one which could be relied on to move in channels in the development of policy which would meet with the approval of the American government and people. The establishment of the Communist regime in the north crystallized the determination of the Military Government in the southern zone not to permit pro-Communist activities in southern Korea. The repressive policies of the North Korean government, which led to a movement of Koreans from the Russian to the American zone, served to lend support, among the South Koreans, to this point of view. For, with all the criticism which developed of American policy, as time went on it became clear that more people wanted to live under even the disturbed conditions which they had created than under the "order" that followed the institution of one-party rule and repression by the Communists.

One reason for the confusion in the American Zone was

"the rapidity with which the way had been opened to the organization of the many political parties which, with freedom of expression and of organization such as the Americans introduced into a country accustomed only to repression, sprang up wholesale around individual leaders. The disorderly and terroristic methods used by the leaders and the parties of the right as well as the left were partly the result of inexperience with democratic methods and partly a carry-over from past experience under a repressive regime. Under the circumstances, responsibility rested with military government rather than with the Koreans, since it alone had the power to enforce more regular procedures. In any case, the outcome was to associate the anti-Communist and conservative Koreans with government in the southern zone while the reverse was occurring in the north. Internal division consequently helped to reenforce that which had been instituted first for military reasons and then maintained because of the growing inability of the Russians and the Americans to agree on the conditions of unification."[44]

Having failed to solve the problem of unification by bilateral agreement and having failed to solve the problem of government unilaterally, in large part because of the division of Korea, as already stated the United States took the Korean question to the United Nations. It took it to the General Assembly rather than the Security Council because of the probability that the Soviet Union would veto decision and action in the Security Council, which it could not do in the General Assembly.

The General Assembly, by a Resolution of November 14, 1947, concluded that the questions at issue should be submitted to freely elected representatives of the Korean people. A United Nations Temporary Commission on Korea was established to observe or supervise the elections. This Commission was "to be present in Korea, with right to travel, observe and consult throughout Korea." Because of Soviet objections,[45] the Commission was not admitted to the northern zone. Consequently the elections of May 10, 1948, were held only in the American zone. These elections the Commission held to have been "a valid expression of the free will of the electorate in those parts of Korea which were accessible to the Commission and in which all of the inhabitants constituted approximately two-thirds of the people of all Korea." The first Congress of the Republic of Korea, thus constituted under United Nations rather than American supervision, proceeded, in consultation with the Temporary Commission, to adopt a constitution, and institute a government to which authority could be transferred by the occupying powers. Under the constitution the Congress, as a constituent assembly, was transformed into a National Assembly to exercise the legislative powers for two years after which new elections would be held as they were in the spring of 1950. It elected Dr. Syngman Rhee as the first President of the Republic, the boundaries of which were defined so as to include all of historic Korea, although in fact the division continued.

Pending consideration by the General Assembly, the United States on August 12, 1948, recognized the new government as being entitled to be regarded as the Government of Korea, envisaged by the General Assembly resolution of November 14, 1947. At the same time China, through the National Government, declared its intention of establishing friendly relations with it, and the Philippine government extended recognition on August 23. The decisions of its Temporary Commission were subsequently upheld by the General Assembly. The Soviet group of states, however, continued to support the northern government so that division was perpetuated.

Transfer of the Korean problem to the United Nations was initially viewed by many as a method of withdrawal by the United States from a weak position. There was withdrawal from the standpoint of the transfer of responsibility from the United States Military Government to the Koreans at a time when it was generally held that, in the event of an early test, the northern government had the power, if it chose to act, to overthrow the southern regime, except as it should be given outside support. There was not withdrawal, however, in the sense that the United States continued to give aid and assistance to the Korean Republic as it was called for.

Nevertheless the ultimate test of American policy, from the standpoint of withdrawal, would come only if and when the Communist regime resorted to force to overthrow the Republic, and then only if it came before the Republic had organized its own power to the point where it could effectively maintain itself.

As it proved, the test came before the government headed by President Rhee had completely stabilized its authority and brought into being the necessary military power to resist attack. Then it was demonstrated that the policy of the United States was, in fact, not one of withdrawal, but one of support of the new regime by military means. But the action taken was on the basis of support of the United Nations rather than ostensibly in implementation of national policy. This was made possible by the earlier transfer of the problem to the General Assembly for solution.

When it was reported on June 25, 1950, that the territories of the Republic had been invaded by the forces of the northern regime, the United States requested an immediate meeting of the Security Council. The Security Council, by a 7 to 1 majority, issued a "cease-fire" order and ordered the retirement of the northern forces back beyond the 38th parallel. Neither order was obeyed. The United States immediately began sending munitions to Korea and soon made clear its intention of giving air and naval support to the Korean government. This was enlarged by July 3 to include support by ground forces. The American actions were approved by the Security Council, which called upon other members of the United Nations to participate in action in support of the Korean Republic. Britain and the Commonwealth Pacific countries immediately put naval forces at the disposal of the United States to assist in maintaining a government which, although not a member of the United Nations, had been established under its auspices; and India, which had first abstained from voting, declared its support of United States and United Nations policy toward Korea.

The Soviet Union was not represented at these meetings of the Security Council, since for some time it had not been attending meetings of United Nations bodies which continued to seat representatives of the Chinese National Government rather than those of the Chinese People's Republic. Subsequently it claimed that all Security Council decisions were illegal because they were not taken with the concurring vote of the five permanent members. The United States view, however, was that it was a Charter obligation for the Security Council to be in continuous session. The refusal of the Soviet government to authorize its representatives to attend could not legally prevent the Council from discharging its functions since that in itself would be a violation of the Charter. The absence of Russia did prevent a veto (or non-concurrence of one of the permanent members) and thus made it possible for action to be taken. But Russian non-representation was viewed by the United States and others as having the same effect as that of abstention from voting, which had come to be used as a way of avoiding association with a decision which the permanent member did not approve but which it was not prepared to veto. But whatever the ultimate conclusion as to legality, it was the policy of the United States to relate its own action to United Nations policy, while insisting on the necessity of action and itself taking action.

This military aggression in Korea had the effect of bringing to a sharp focus what had been tendencies toward change in American Far Eastern policy. This may most readily be seen through an examination of the postwar policy of the United States toward Japan.

5. *Postwar Policy Toward Japan*

The war policy defined by the United States for Japan was that of "unconditional surrender." What the Japanese should understand their unconditional surrender to mean was stated in general terms in the Potsdam Proclamation of July 26, 1945. This Proclamation by the United States, Britain, and China, however, expressed Allied policy and not a commitment to Japan. Since an undifferentiated group called the Japanese militarists were viewed as being responsible for Japan's policies of military aggrandizement, the Proclamation naturally stated that "There must be eliminated for all time the authority and influence of those who have deceived and misled the people of Japan into embarking on world conquest." This militarism was to be destroyed although

"We do not intend that the Japanese shall be enslaved as a race or destroyed as a nation, but stern justice shall be meted out to all war criminals, including those who have visited cruelties upon our prisoners. The Japanese government shall remove all obstacles to the revival and strengthening of democratic tendencies among the Japanese people. Freedom of speech, of religion, and of thought, as well as respect for the fundamental human rights shall be established.

"Japan shall be permitted to maintain such industries as will sustain her economy and permit the exaction of just reparations in kind, but not those which would permit her to re-arm for war. To this end, access to, as distinguished from control of, raw materials shall be permitted."

The means to be employed to attain the Allied objectives were stated to be: (1) occupation "of points in Japanese territory to be designated by the Allies," but with the occupying forces to be withdrawn from Japan "as soon as these objectives have been accomplished and there has been established in accordance with the freely expressed will of the Japanese people a peacefully inclined and responsible government;" (2) by implication, the use of the Japanese government as an instrument of rule; and (3) the limitation of Japan's sovereignty "to the islands of Honshu, Hokkaido, Kyushu, Shikoku and such minor islands as we determine."

It was American policy to keep the control of Japan during the period of occupation in its own hands, even though the occupation was formally established as an Allied operation. Thus an American, General of the Army Douglas MacArthur, was designated by the United States as the Supreme Commander for the Allied Powers (S.C.A.P.). Concurrently he was designated Commander-in-Chief of the American Far East Command with headquarters in Tokyo. This was the main force of the occupation, the other Allies participating only through what were in essence token forces. Suggestions, as the Russian, that Japan be divided into zones for military occupation purposes, were not accepted, so that occupied Japan was maintained as an entity, with the Headquarters established by the Supreme Commander exercising authority directly over all occupation forces. The initial statement of post-surrender policy for Japan was that prepared jointly by the State, War, and Navy Departments of the American government, which was approved by the President on September 6, 1945. This basic policy document was substantially re-affirmed by the Far Eastern Commission as the "Basic Post-Surrender Policy for Japan" on June 19, 1947, but until that reaffirmation occupation policy was based upon the expressed views of the United States government, formulated and applied unilaterally.

Before the signature of the surrender instruments, however, "the United States suggested that there be created an international body to help formulate future policy in Japan and to assist in planning the organization which would be required to make sure that the Japanese fulfilled their obligations."[46] What was in mind was a purely advisory commission. The Soviet government refused to participate in such a commission, but an agreement was reached at the Moscow Conference of Foreign Ministers (December 27, 1945) on the constitution of the Far Eastern Commission (F.E.C.), with eleven states to be represented, to sit in Washington, and of an advisory council, the Allied Council for Japan, composed of representatives of the four major Pacific powers (the U.S.S.R., China, Britain and the Pacific Commonwealth, and the United States), to sit in Tokyo. This organization modified the American character of the occupation but did not serve fundamentally to change it since the terms of reference of the Allied bodies were designed to ensure that final decision on policy should rest with the American Government or with S.C.A.P.

As previously stated, pre-surrender policy implied the application of the surrender terms through the Japanese government. The post-surrender policy statement made this explicit.

> "In view of the present character of Japanese society and the desire of the United States to attain its objectives with a minimum commitment of

its forces and resources, the Supreme Commander will exercise his authority through Japanese governmental machinery and agencies, including the Emperor, to the extent that this satisfactorily furthers United States objectives. The Japanese Government will be permitted, under his instructions, to exercise the normal powers of government in matters of domestic administration. This policy, however, will be subject to the right and duty of the Supreme Commander to require changes in governmental machinery or personnel or to act directly if the Emperor or other Japanese authority does not satisfactorily meet the requirements of the Supreme Commander in effectuating the surrender terms. This policy, moreover, does not commit the Supreme Commander to support the Emperor or any other Japanese governmental authority in opposition to evolutionary changes looking toward the attainment of United States objectives. The policy is to use the existing form of Government in Japan, not to support it. Changes in the form of Government initiated by the Japanese people or government in the direction of modifying its feudal and authoritarian tendencies are to be permitted and favored. In the event that the effectuation of such changes involves the use of force by the Japanese people or government against persons opposed thereto, the Supreme Commander should intervene only when necessary to ensure the security of his forces and the attainment of all other objectives of the occupation."[47]

The United States' substantive policy, as defined in directives which were interpreted and implemented by S.C.A.P.

either directly or through the Japanese government, was to bring about: (a) the disarmament of Japan and the repatriation and demobilization of the Japanese military forces; (b) the demilitarization of Japan, (1) economically, through the destruction of the existing economic basis of Japanese military strength and the prevention of its revival and (2) politically, through the elimination of all military and para-military organizations in the country and through the elimination from the educational system of all militarist and ultra-nationalist emphases; (c) the trial and punishment of all war criminals and the elimination from positions of authority of all those who had held positions from which they had influenced or could influence policy in the direction of war and aggression; (d) the payment of reparations "through the transfer . . . of Japanese property located outside of the territories to be retained by Japan, and through the transfer of such goods or existing capital equipment and facilities as are not necessary for a peaceful Japanese economy or the supplying of the occupation forces"; and (e) the encouragement of democratization by the negative action of removal of legal obstructions on freedom of speech and organization and positive action looking toward political, economic, and social change.

In the execution of this program, the repatriation of troops and their demobilization, together with disarmament, were rapidly and efficiently carried through. The seal was set on disarmament and this aspect of demilitarization by provisions of the 1947 Japanese Constitution stipulating that "land, sea and air forces, as well as other military potential will never be maintained," and eliminating the War and Navy departments from the structure of government. An International War Crimes Tribunal set up in Tokyo had, by the end of 1948, tried and set punishments for those found guilty of war crimes, under a sufficiently broad definition of war crimes to bring under the jurisdiction of the Tribunal such high officials of government as Marquis Koichi Kido, Lord Keeper of the Privy Seal, Yosuke Matsuoka, former Minister of Foreign Affairs, and Kiichiro Hiranuma, ex-President of the Privy Council, in addition to General Hideki Tojo, ex-Premier, and others. In addition to the trial of war criminals, purges were instituted, designed to remove from participation in government first, and subsequently in industry, those who had any important relationship to the formulation of Japan's war policies.

In addition to measures related to the liquidation of the war, S.C.A.P. undertook an extensive program of political, social, and economic reform, going beyond "encouragement" of any reformative tendencies shown by the Japanese government or people. These included: replacement of the Meiji constitution with the constitution of 1947; reform within the administrative structure of government; enlargement of the electorate through the introduction of woman's suffrage; revival of popular political activity through the medium of political parties; encouragement of unionization of labor and labor activity along American lines; reform of the educational system; land reform in the interest of reduction of the amount of tenancy and absentee landlordism; and changes in the industrial structure through the breakup of the Zaibatsu and the deconcentration of industry program.

It is unnecessary for present purposes to review this reform program in any detail. It is only necessary to note that the Supreme Commander interpreted his directives as requiring or justifying a wide program of reform, whether or not initiated by the Japanese government. Thus it may be concluded that it was United States policy to use the period of the occupation to bring about changes in the direction of political and economic democratization which would have some element of permanence. An essentially conservative

Japanese government was utilized by S.C.A.P. as the instruments of such reform as seemed to him necessary.

The emphasis on reform, however, began to decrease after 1947. At a press conference in the spring of that year, General MacArthur characterized the occupation as having virtually attained Allied objectives, except in relation to economic recovery, which, he held, could best be accomplished by an independent Japan. Acceptance of this view led the United States to initiate a movement looking toward an early peace treaty with Japan. The proposals made by the United States for a conference among the Allies to work out a permanent peace settlement, however, proved unacceptable to the Soviet Union and, partly because of Soviet objections, to China. Chinese compromise proposals also proved unacceptable. The Soviet government was unwilling to concede the right of the states represented on the Far Eastern Commission to participate in the negotiations on an equality with the United States, the Soviet Union, Britain, and China. It held that the making of peace treaties was a function of the Foreign Ministers of those states, with other interested states limited to an advisory role.

If a peace treaty had been negotiated in 1947, or even in 1948, its terms would have been based upon the view then held in the United States as well as elsewhere that the existing condition of disarmament of Japan should be perpetuated. Since this would have left Japan defenseless against external aggression, responsibility for Japan's security would have had to be devolved either on other states or on the United Nations. Furthermore the government of a disarmed Japan would, under existing conditions, have lacked the power to maintain itself against internal subversion. In addition, an independent Japan might have had to face unaided the problem of revival and reconstruction of its economic life for, as of 1947, little progress had been made toward the

restoration of production to the level of the years 1930-1934
—the prewar norm which had been set by the Far Eastern
Commission. In other words, the movement toward a peace
treaty was initiated at a time when it was assumed to be consistent with American interests to withdraw from a Japan
which could not be expected to maintain its own security,
much less to play a power role in the politics of the Far East.

Since Soviet action prevented the realization of the American objective with respect to a termination of the occupation,
American policy toward Japan began to change from reforms
which had at least a short-run weakening effect on the country,
especially economically, to an emphasis on economic recovery
and reconstruction.

"At the beginning of 1948, the United States representative on the Far Eastern Commission, on the basis of a review
of development, made it clear that the United States had
come to the conclusion that more direct and energetic measures should be taken by SCAP to bring about the industrial
recovery of Japan, since that had not been accomplished by
the Japanese themselves."[48] The initial view on which
S.C.A.P. had operated was that

> "The plight of Japan is the direct outcome of its
> own behavior, and the Allies will not undertake
> the burden of repairing the damage. . . .
>
> "Japan will be expected to provide goods and
> services to meet the needs of the occupying forces
> to the extent that this can be effected without caus-
> ing starvation, wide-spread disease and acute physi-
> cal distress.
>
> "The Japanese authorities will be expected, and
> if necessary directed, to maintain, develop and en-
> force programs that serve the following purposes:
>
> "(a) To avoid acute economic distress.

"(b) To assure just and impartial distribution of available supplies.

"(c) To meet the requirements for reparations deliveries agreed upon by the Allied Governments.

"(d) To facilitate the restoration of the Japanese economy so that the reasonable peaceful requirements of the population can be satisfied."[49]

The Japanese, but only with substantial American assistance, were able to restore their economy sufficiently so as to "avoid acute economic distress," and "to meet the needs of the occupying forces." But, even before the formalization of the new policy, they had not been required to "meet the requirements for reparations deliveries." Those requirements were constantly scaled down, while

"plant and tool production facilities originally earmarked for removal on the basis of the findings of the Pauley Commission were not only not removed from Japan but much of it was gradually brought back into use on the ground that specific plants were needed in production in order to meet requirements in production set by SCAP. Reports made by subsequent investigators of Japan's own requirements were the basis for modification downward of the Pauley Report. In consequence, by August, 1948, SCAP reports showed a shipment out of Japan to advance transfer claimants of only some 18,000 machine tools, of a weight of under 60,000 metric tons."[50]

Under the new policy of bringing back Japanese industrial production to the prewar level, the policy of requiring reparations vanished completely.

The assumption of responsibility for restoring Japan's economy to the level of 1930-1934 (according to the F.E.C.),

or 1932-1936 (according to S.C.A.P.), first limited the reform emphasis and then led to a change of policy wherever
implementation of a specific reform had an adverse effect
on production. It also focused attention on the problem
of foreign trade, since Japan's industrial development had
been made possible by the processing of imported raw materials. Steps had been begun in the second half of 1947
looking toward the reinstitution of foreign trade, with increased private participation, instead of handling it entirely on
a governmental basis through S.C.A.P. If the prewar situation was to be reproduced, however, either through Japanese
government efforts or as a result of S.C.A.P. activity, it would
have to be by decreasing Japan's abnormal trade dependence
on the United States and reestablishing the trade conditions
of the 1930-1934 period, when Japan secured 24 per
cent of her imports from the United States and 53 per cent
from Asia (excluding Australia), and shipped 23 per cent
of her exports to the United States, 60 per cent to Asia.
This contrasts with the 1947 figures, when Japan obtained
92 per cent of her imports from the United States and only
6 per cent from Asia, sending only 12 per cent of her exports
to the United States and 66 per cent to Asia.

The new United States policy of seeking to reestablish
Japan's economic strength at the 1930-1934 level, where
it was expected that Japan would be at least self-supporting,
produced dissatisfaction in some Far Eastern countries. These
nations remembered that in the early thirties Japan was
economically the most powerful Far Eastern state, able to
exercise, by economic means, considerable influence in Eastern
and Southeastern Asia. This dissatisfaction made them cau-
tious of accepting American proposals with respect to a peace
treaty. The implication they saw in the new policy, which,
in addition to its emphasis on economic recovery, was directed
toward the transfer of the internal powers of government to

the Japanese, was that the United States proposed to build Japan into an ally rather than to continue to occupy her as an enemy state.

There were several reasons why the war-engendered attitude of the United States toward Japan and the Japanese changed. Unquestionably, one was the unexpectedly complaisant attitude of the Japanese toward the occupation and its personnel. Another was a reflection, on the part of Americans, of lessened esteem for Kuomintang China, which revived the prewar attitude of friendliness toward Japan as a country of domestic order and general tidiness, and one which showed a greater appreciation of the techniques and scientific methodology of the West. The apparent eagerness with which the Japanese sought, under directive, to make themselves over in the American democratic image helped to revive and fix the view of Japan as a country to be trusted and assisted.

But fundamentally the change in American policy was a reflection of political change. At the end of World War II, American Far Eastern policy was based upon the view that postwar China would become the stable leading power in the Far East and that China would be unified and stabilized under a government friendly to the United States, which would act with the United States in case of conflict in the area. On this assumption, a relatively weak Japan, completely friendly to the United States or not, would be tolerable and could be required to play a passive role in Far Eastern politics.

By 1948, however, it seemed to be clear that, at the best, China would remain a problem in Far Eastern politics and would not be able to contribute to the maintenance of peace and order in the area. Regardless of the outcome of its internal struggle, it was doubtful whether the China which would emerge from the civil war would be especially friendly toward the United States. In and after 1947, furthermore, such ten-

sion had developed in the relations of the United States and
the Soviet Union that other questions of policy were more and
more subordinated to the effect of decisions on the relations
and relative power of those two states. When the outcome
of the struggle in China could be forecast as favorable to the
Communists (a forecast that had been made even earlier)
China was eliminated as a base for American Far Eastern
policy in the struggle against the Soviet Union. Instead of
the China which was unified being under a friendly government, it was under an avowedly hostile one. And just as the
early policy toward Japan was a reflection of policy toward
China, so, as the situation in China changed, did American
policy toward Japan.

Thus, in relation to the problem of containing Soviet expansion, Japan came to be viewed in American defense policy
as the northern anchor of the defense system. This conception, together with changed conditions on the continent of
Asia, necessitated a reexamination of the question of a peace
treaty and of its terms. The state of relations with the Soviet
Union seemed to preclude a treaty along the lines originally
contemplated, which would have been designed to perpetu-
ate Japan's military and economic weakness. A Japan
independent but in that condition would have been open to
ready conquest, either by direct attack or by internal subversion by the Japanese Communist Party, supported from
the mainland. A treaty which would enable Japan to be developed, or to develop herself, into a power factor in the Far
East aligned in interest and sympathy with the United States
could not be expected to prove acceptable to the Soviet Union
or to China, if the Communist regime should be recognized as entitled to formulate the will of China in place of
the National Government.

Consequently, the question being debated early in 1950
was the feasibility of ending the occupation by means of a

treaty accepted by the United States and some, but not all, of the states represented on the Far Eastern Commission. The Japanese had been led to hope for and anticipate a treaty early in 1950 which would terminate the occupation. It was argued that the effect of not concluding one would be to make them unfriendly to the United States, thus playing into the hands of the Communist opposition.

General MacArthur had apparently not moved during 1949 from the views (as to the need for an early treaty) which he had expressed in 1947. Similarly the Department of State continued its exploration of the possibility of meeting what had come to be considered a demand of the Japanese and also of S.C.A.P. On the other hand, the Defense Department, on grounds of national security, was apparently moving toward the view that the occupation, on the military side, should be maintained, or that a treaty should be negotiated only if it gave the United States military bases and facilities in Japan similar to those granted by the Philippines.

Whether or not because of the revelation of the maintenance of working relations between the Japanese Communist Party and the Cominform and because of increasingly vigorous Soviet criticism of aspects of S.C.A.P. policy (both of which produced a strong reaction from S.C.A.P., and the former from the Japanese government), S.C.A.P. moved toward the Defense Department point of view in the spring of 1950. The policy which was emerging thus apparently was one of maintaining, with the concurrence of the Japanese government, the military side of the occupation represented by the Far East Command, while ending as rapidly as possible the remaining non-military activities of S.C.A.P., thus restoring self-control to Japan except with respect to national defense and foreign affairs.

The invasion of the Korean Republic by the forces of the Communist North Korean People's Republic crystallized

American policy toward Japan along the above-mentioned lines, at least for the time being. It was from Japan that American assistance was sent to South Korea under the orders of President Truman, in the form first of munitions and air support, and then of American ground forces. The Korean operation was brought under the command of General Mac-Arthur, with his Headquarters remaining in Japan. Thus, under emergency conditions, the advantage of the maintenance of American forces in Japan was demonstrated.

Similarly, the outbreak in Korea also crystallized, although in at least one case in the form of apparent reversal of policy, other aspects of United States Far Eastern policy. The most apparent reversal was in the case of Formosa, with the sending of the Seventh Fleet to the Straits with orders to prevent a Communist invasion of the island. Even here, however, there was crystallization as well as reversal, since it was declared that title to the island could not be fixed until there was security in the Pacific, a peace treaty with Japan, or a decision by the United Nations, and since the move was not an affirmative one in support of Chiang Kai-shek but rather a negative one to prevent the extension of Sovietism. Beyond this, the commitment to aid France in its support of the Bao Dai government against the Communist-led Viet Minh Party was reaffirmed and extended, and a firmer policy of support of the Philippine government was expressed, together with an intention to strengthen American forces in the Islands. The new policy also committed the United States to support the other governments in Southeast Asia against Communist-promoted disorder.

Thus the outbreak of the Korean war had a much broader effect on American policy than that of support of the Korean Republic. The debate over the failures of the policy followed in China led to a reexamination of the "country" aspects of Far Eastern policy, with a view to the definition of an overall

Far Eastern policy within which there could be correlation and coordination of the lines of specific "country" policies. The new overall policy for Eastern Asia is that earlier formulated with respect to the Middle East and Europe of the "containment of Communism." Briefly, this means preventing the direct or indirect extension of Soviet power and influence beyond its present limits through the use of American resources and, if necessary, American military power.

6. American Policy, 1949-1950

On the basis of a review of American Far Eastern policy, especially since 1945, the conclusion must be drawn that policy has followed change rather than anticipating it. One reason for this has been the development and application of policy on hypotheses or assumptions the validity of which was not subjected to constant reexamination. One assumption which affected American policy in the Far East as well as in Europe was that the Soviet Union would conduct its foreign relations more or less within the accepted limits of diplomatic propriety, so that policy conflicts could be adjusted by the use of normal methods of negotiation. This assumption involved cooperation between the major states on the premise that through cooperation the conditions of a stable peace could and would be found. This had to be tried out as a working hypothesis if World War II was not to be immediately transformed into World War III. It was first tested in Europe, in the attempts to negotiate the conditions of peace with Italy, Austria, and Germany itself. A basis of accommodation became increasingly difficult to find except as the United States was prepared to make concessions without equivalent Russian concessions. Secretary Byrnes made a slight modification of the initial conciliatory American attitude when he stipulated that the American method of dealing with Russia must be one of firmness coupled with patience in negotiation, and adjustment of policy necessary to meet accusations of "softness" already leveled against the Roosevelt administration because of the concessions at Yalta. Under Secretary Marshall and Secretary Acheson the shift went further, to the point of a policy of no negotiation without prior evidence given by the Russians of willingness to reach agreement and of intention to observe agreements reached by negotiation, through observing those already concluded. This in effect meant rejection of the initial hypothesis on which policy was constructed and applied. That hypothesis had been crystallized, however, in the thinking of a segment of the American public. The carry-over obstructed the rapid unification of public opinion in support of policy based upon the new hypothesis, again developed and applied in Europe.

The new assumption was that before the Soviet Union could be brought to a willingness to cooperate, its power would have to be "contained." Thus, under the "Truman Doctrine," announced on March 12, 1947,

> "The Soviet Government and the world were given to understand that we would oppose further extension of Soviet control, by negotiation or penetration or force, into western Germany, western Austria, Italy, Greece, Turkey or the Middle East. . . . The events of the past two years had seemed to prove that the Soviets would continue to push outward at this or that point in the perimeter of their 'empire' until they were blocked by the application of counterforce, and that the United States was the only power capable of applying such counterforce."[51]

The methods of Soviet expansion were such, however, that they could not readily be met by the "application of counterforce" in the normal military fashion, for Soviet expansion was not attempted by direct military means resulting in international war. Rather, use was made of national Communist parties, whose policies the Kremlin was able to dictate because of the conditions of operation of the Comintern and its postwar successor, the Cominform. The method was that of movement toward control through stimulating and capitalizing on internal disorders in some countries or, where it could be secured, through control of key posts in coalition governments. This presented the new problem of preventing extension of Soviet control rather than the normal one of checking attempts at expansion by direct action, whether economic or military. The problem was essentially that of applying the counterforce in such a way as to avoid undue interference in the internal affairs of the threatened states.

Given the nature of this problem, it was a short step from the Truman Doctrine to the Marshall Plan. It was easier to take this step, and to obtain American public support for it, than would otherwise have been the case, because the Marshall Plan was in effect a projection into the new postwar situation of the already established assumption of American responsibility to assist in the reconstruction of wartorn Europe, but on a basis of sharing the burden with those who could assist themselves and one another. At any rate, the Marshall Plan offered the possibility of preventing the extension of Soviet control by developing a greater measure of economic stability in threatened states. Improved economic conditions, it was reasoned, would make it less possible for Communist parties to capitalize politically on impoverishment and unemployment, which breed unrest and disorder.

The Marshall Plan approach was evolved slowly because it had to be preceded by the discussion in Congress and in the country necessary to win acceptance of the idea that commitments of such magnitude were in the national interest and within the limits of reasonable possibility, so far as the burden on the American economy was concerned. The nature of the European Recovery Program and of the similarly motivated Greek aid program required Congressional rather than purely executive action. It thus necessarily enhanced the factor of public discussion in the formulation and application of foreign policy, bringing the House of Representatives into a more influential position and enlarging and changing the nature of the role of the Senate. This, in turn, brought foreign policy even more into the area of party controversy than it had been in the past. But, except for the slowing effects involved in debate, an adjustment to the new situation was made through projecting into American United Nations and European policy the technique of bipartisanship in the formulation of policy. This had been emphasized by Secretary Hull in an approach to the development of international organization. The bipartisan approach, where used, helped to hold discussion within proper limits. It was not, however, applied universally; and thus, with respect to policy outside the area of agreement on its applicability, and particularly concerning Far Eastern policy, the way was left open for debate designed to secure partisan advantage.

As the Marshall Plan for Europe began to be put into effect, it naturally emphasized the unity of interest of the European states which voluntarily came within the framework of the Plan. The conditions of its application also led to the broadening of American policy from the economic to the political and military spheres, culminating in the Atlantic Pact. In this connection it is particularly significant that the tendency in policy was from the use of economic means, without military commitment, to the recognition of advance military commitments as part of the program of containment of Soviet expansion in Europe. This somewhat parallels the shift in emphasis in the program for Greece, in which initially the priority was also put on economic means although there was a secondary acceptance of responsibility for military assistance from the beginning.

(a) Differences Between American Policies Toward Europe and Toward Asia

These developments in the field of European policy did not find a concurrent expression in the Far East. Except incidentally, this was true even with respect to the initial assumption as to the need for Great Power cooperation in the taking of decisions. An exception was made respecting Korea. As previously suggested, it was understood that the Soviet Union was prepared to acquiesce in unilateral action by the United States in an attempt to bring about an acceptable solution of the internal situation in China. Also, as suggested above, the United States, in fact if not in theory, reserved to itself the power to decide and implement policy on Japan. It supported diplomatically the policy of cooperation in Eastern Europe, where it had the least power to act in support of the policy. In the area of its greatest power, where it sought to move unilaterally, it failed to appreciate the fact that Russia was in a position to act as the United States was not in the sphere which the Soviet had preempted as its own. From this standpoint, to be sure, the comparison is closer to Western than to Eastern Europe. However, the power position in the Far East was obscured by acceptance of the assumption that the Soviet government had formulated its requirements, which had been met at Yalta, and that beyond them it would follow American leadership in the area.

A similarity between Europe and the Far East in American policy, up to and even after the coup d'état in Czechoslovakia, was the failure to appreciate the position of national Communist parties in their relationship to the Kremlin and as instruments of Soviet foreign policy. The Chinese Communist Party was too long viewed as essentially a party of agrarian reform, which would participate in national politics within a democratic framework. It was on this view that American policy toward China was first based. After that view was no longer tenable, those whose knowledge of China was held to be unquestionable argued that the Chinese Communist Party, even viewed as Communist in its program, was fundamentally nationalist and thus would not accept outside direction, as had Communist parties in other countries. In short, it was held that the nature of China and of the Chinese was such that the word to be underscored in the term Chinese Communist was *Chinese* rather than *Communist*.

The combination of these two points of view brought the conclusion that the outcome of the internal struggle for power in China, whatever it should prove to be, would not have dangerous consequences for the United States in its struggle to contain Soviet power. Consequently American support of the National Government against the Communists, while extensive, was never designed to be great enough to force a decision favorable to it as essential to the interests of the United States. But in the United States there was sufficient underlying fear of Communism to make it politically hazardous for the government to withdraw its support completely and openly from the Kuomintang and transfer it to the Communists. As the situation developed, the divisions in American opinion on China policy, or perhaps more accurately the confusion as to policy, brought the State Department under a crossfire of criticism which made an honest reexamination of China policy in terms of the national interest difficult.

(b) Support of Nationalist China

In this connection, it must be recalled that the conclusion had been reached that the Kuomintang and thus the National Government, with its existing personnel, was not an effective instrument of rule or for the accomplishment of democratic reform and economic reconstruction. Considerable criticism had been made of the Greek aid program as having the effect of commiting the United States to the support of an unpopular, "reactionary," and essentially ineffective government. The same general argument could be made with respect to the support of some existing regimes in the Far Eastern countries. The governments through which assistance in reconstruction would have to be given, if given at all, in a number of countries, were not of a kind in which Americans could have the same confidence, from the standpoint of an established tradition of democratic action and of reasonably effective government, as it could have in the governments of western Europe which came within the European assistance program. In the latter case there was reason to believe that assistance given would lead to the planned result. In the former case it was argued that only a small part of American aid would be applied to attain the desired end. A large part of it, it was anticipated, would be diverted to serve personal and private ends. The point of view which came to be widely held with respect to proposals for a large-scale Marshall Plan type of program for China and the Far East was that summed up in the charge that it would be pouring money needed elsewhere "down the drain."

To a degree, however, this was a rationalization of the negative aspects of Far Eastern policy rather than the reason for them. The European program was taking a large slice of the not unlimited national income. Those who were responsible for the development of policy and also of opinion in the country were committed to the view that Europe was the decisive area in the growing conflict between the United States and the Soviet Union. With this emphasis on Europe, it could only be expected that both attention and assistance would be focused on Europe and that there would be reluctance to divert American energy and resources from the European program should such diversion be necessary to implement Far Eastern policy. Consequently all reasonable excuses for limitation of action in the Far East were seized upon. On the other hand, it should be recognized that some of those who were opposed to the European program, but who did not feel it expedient to oppose it publicly, seized upon the situation in China and in Southeastern Asia to urge the curtailment even below the limits of effectiveness of authorizations for expenditure in Europe, ostensibly because there was no comparable program for Asia. Their activity—which supported the views of those who, as more or less professional friends of the China which they identified as the Kuomintang and personified in Chiang Kai-shek, demanded all-out aid to prevent the Communist conquest of China—secured a limited E.C.A. program for China, but too limited and too late significantly to affect the outcome of the civil war.

A European type program, in any case, could not be established for the Far East until general purposes could be defined for the entire area and agreement reached on the program and on its application with the other parties in interest. There had been a program of assistance to China which by midsummer of 1949 was officially declared to have been ineffective. The occupation of Japan had entailed relatively large expenditures for relief and rehabilitation purposes, but these were unrelated to the general purposes of the China program. For special reasons there had been a Philippine assistance program, the justification for which was unrelated to the China problem or that in Japan. And there was no agreement with the countries of Southeastern Asia, Australia, the Philippines, Britain, and Holland on concerted action to "contain" Communism, even though there were Communist attempts to exploit the nationalist ferment in Southeast Asia, and despite the fact that there was an obvious even though limited relationship between the recovery of some of the European countries and the establishment of stability and consequent revival of production in the old colonial area.

President Truman's Point Four proposal, although not made directly as part of an overall program for the containment of Communism in the Far East, pointed a finger in that direction, since it looked toward planned action designed to raise the productivity and the standard of living of underdeveloped countries. If that could be done in, for example, the countries of Southeastern Asia, the instability resulting from economic backwardness and distress would be gradually lessened and thus, in terms of the argument in support of the Marshall Plan, the countries affected would be less fertile ground for the cultivation of Communism.

But because such a program could be viewed as representing a move in the cold war between the United States and the Soviet Union, countries desirous of remaining neutral in the struggle because of the possible adverse consequences of taking sides were reluctant to associate themselves even with a program of development sponsored by the United States.

(c) The Position of India

The most important neutral among the states of eastern Asia was India. It is beyond the scope of this book to review Indian policy or the policy of the United States toward India. It may be noted, however, that India's policy was one of neutrality as between the United States and the Soviet Union. Within the limits set by that policy, India began immediately after it had become independent to seek to play a leading role in Asian politics, especially with respect to Southeast Asia. In this respect it did not conceive of neutrality as involving abstention from participation in international affairs, even when it was not a direct party in interest. Thus, through such discussions as the Asian Relations Conference of 1947, it sought to stimulate the development of an inter-Asian point of view on economic questions and on political questions related to colonialism. In the latter connection it is only necessary to recall the initiative taken by India, together with Australia, in bringing the Indonesian question before the United Nations Security Council.

But the possibility of assertion of leadership in the Far East by India was qualified by two factors: (1) its unwillingness to lead in relation to questions where its neutrality might be prejudiced in the view of either the United States or the Soviet Union; and (2) its necessary preoccupation with internal problems, including those involved in its relations with Pakistan. Its own internal weaknesses, its unsettled relations with Pakistan, and its fears, based on its location, of the Soviet Union, were factors in the establishment of the policy of neutrality. Consequently India did not attempt to put itself at the head of an organized Asian bloc which had its own program of development to present to the United States. Its neutrality reflected weakness rather than the strength which would enable it to lead or even to mediate between the Communists and the anti-Communists in the Far East.

The major suggestion from the Far East which had relevance to the American-Soviet conflict, and which might have had a different reception if it had won unqualified Indian support, was that sponsored in 1949 by the Philippine President, Quirino (in consultation with Chiang Kai-shek and the Korean President, Syngman Rhee), of a Pacific Regional Security Pact, bringing together all of the anti-Communist elements in the Far East. This was viewed by the United States as enlarging its responsibilities, if it encouraged such a program or participated in it, without any notable strengthening of the American position.

(d) Reexamination and Criticisms of United States Policy

It was, however, in 1949 that the United States began a reexamination of its "country" policies with a view to the definition of an overall Far Eastern policy, within which existing contradictions in policy could be eliminated. The first step in this direction was the publication by the Department of State of the China White Paper, designed to close the chapter on support of the Kuomintang so as to open the way for a fresh approach to the China problem. This was followed by the appointment of a committee of consultants, under Ambassador-at-Large Philip C. Jessup, with the function of reappraisal and reorientation. During the period of the committee's examination of the problem, both in the United States and in conferences of Foreign Service and Department officers at Bangkok and elsewhere, the whole complex of problems, including definition of objectives and of methods of attaining them, received much press attention and discussion in the United States.

The focal point of public discussion, however, was not the problem of constructing a new policy or policies adapted to the changed situation in the Far East, but responsibility for the failure of the policies which had been followed in China. It was obviously essential to establish the reasons for failure and the extent of failure of one method of solution as part of the process of definition of methods which would have a greater possibility of success. Thus, if the reason for failure was the inherent weaknesses of the Kuomintang and the Generalissimo, as found in the White Paper, then obviously success could not be expected through continued support of the Generalissimo. If the probable ineffectiveness of Japan as a base was found to be the result of application of certain policies followed by the occupation authorities, that finding would have to be made as part of the process of developing a new policy which would make Japan effective.

But the focus on responsibility was quite different from this sort of examination of the reasons for success or failure. Since Far Eastern policy had been developed by a Democratic administration, without close consultation as to its nature and direction with the Republican party leadership, its failures were open to partisan attack to a greater extent than would have been the case if it had been developed and applied within the framework of bipartisanship. Thus, appraisal by critics was primarily directed toward embarrassing and weakening the administration rather than toward establishing sound lines of future development.

Since the cold war and the Russian methods of waging it abroad had focused attention on and developed fears of internal subversion, one line of attack on the formulators of policy was that they had established a direct or indirect association with Communist-front organizations in the United States. This tactic was used to the maximum by Senator McCarthy of Wisconsin in forcing the issue before a subcommittee of the Senate (Tydings Committee). His premises were simple. They were that the State Department had made the China policy and was consequently responsible for its failure. The State Department, Senator McCarthy charged, was packed with Communist sympathizers. Therefore its policy had been constructed deliberately along lines favorable to the Communists and thus designed to meet Soviet rather than American requirements. It was not the complexity and the difficulty of the problem which was responsible for the failure to find the right solutions; failure was designed by the "architects" of the policy.

Of course, the ultimate responsibility rested with the President. There was no credible basis for a direct attack on him along this line. Secretary of State Acheson, however, was in a more vulnerable position, as he had never had occasion to establish a strong political position for himself and had made references as a loyal personal friend to a person (Alger Hiss) found guilty of perjury in connection with a charge of Communist activities while in the State Department. The direct charge of Communist affiliation could not be sustained against

Secretary Acheson, so it had to be centered elsewhere but where he could be associated with the charge by virtue of his responsible position, and so that through him the ultimate target, the President, could be reached with a view to weakening him and his party in domestic politics. The actual center of attack could never be effectively localized since the McCarthy tactics proved to be those of the grasshopper. He jumped rapidly from one name to another, so that the inquiry could never keep up with the accusations, none of which seemed, however, to be sustained with proof.

These attacks, however, apart from the unjustified damage to individuals, had certain consequences. The first was the creation of a popular presumption that there must be a bad situation, even though it could not be defined, in the Department of State. The second was that public attention was completely diverted from consideration of the problems of policy, since the issue had been shifted from the field of policy to that of personalities and from that of personalities to that of association with Communism, without regard to the time of association or of its relevance to the redefinition of Far Eastern policy. A third consequence was that those who bore responsibility for making recommendations in the field of policy tended inevitably to be inhibited from honest analysis and evaluation. A fourth consequence was the weakening of the standing abroad of responsible American officials because of the defensive positions which they had to take at home. The extent to which the charges were made with a view to affecting the political climate in the United States in anticipation of elections, and consequently their real motivation, was not always appreciated in many parts of the world or among those unfamiliar with the processes of American politics. Thus, at both ends of the diplomatic line development of policy was slowed up, and the moral authority of the United States was weakened in a period of crisis.

(e) Containment of Soviet Expansion

The real problem, from which the attention of the American people tended to be diverted by the McCarthy "show" and by the "side-shows" connected with it, was the question of method, means, and place of establishment of the line of containment of Soviet expansion through the utilization of national Communist parties. The limits which that expansion of power had reached by 1950 were roughly continental and inclusive of eastern Asiatic territories down to Indo-China, with the exception of Korea south of the 38th parallel. A qualification of this generalization would be found in the existence within China of pockets of resistance, including in total fairly large elements which the Communists labeled "bandits," but which the National Government claimed as guerrillas responsive to its direction. If the implementation of the policy of containment required a reduction of the area of Communist control, then the question to which an answer had to be found was whether resistance movements within China proper could be effectively supported from outside, and if so, how, and through whom? The only apparently available medium was the National Government on Formosa. But the effectiveness of action through that instrumentality had already been brought into question. Furthermore, there was no available evidence to support the view that those who were maintaining resistance to the Communists in China aimed to reinstitute Kuomintang rule. And there was also a question, which the State Department tended to answer in the negative, as to the ability of Chiang Kai-shek even to maintain himself unaided against a Communist attack on Formosa itself. The failure to hold Hainan Island, and the conditions of that failure, underscored the weakness rather than the recuperative capacity of the Formosa regime.

If containment meant acceptance of the continental extension of Soviet influence to the point reached by early 1950, but establishment of a defensible line beyond which it would not be permitted to go, the problem became one of determining the positions which could be maintained, or which must be maintained, both on and off the continent. Here policy had to be approached in terms of the probable and possible rather than in terms of abstract desires. The American position in Korea, Japan, the Philippines (with Formosa in between), Indo-China, and Southeastern Asia had to be reappraised from both political and military standpoints.

The conclusion which must be drawn from actions taken before war broke out is that Southern Korea was initially viewed as being beyond the line of military containment. On the same basis, the conclusion must be reached that it was thought possible to establish the authority of the Bao Dai government in Indo-China, and thus to prevent any southward continental expansion of the Communist area. Shifts in occupation policy in Japan, and the movement away from the idea of an early treaty on terms which would give Japan independence and preclude the maintenance of American military forces and bases there, indicated that the Japanese islands would be used as the northern anchor of a containment line extending south to include the Philippines. Policy toward Formosa remained unresolved.

Beyond this position, the great question was whether or not the United States would commit itself, or was even moving toward a commitment, to prepare and to use military means if necessary to prevent the extension of Soviet power into one or another of the areas mentioned, unless the Soviet Union itself acted directly. The discussions centered on the organization and utilization of economic means to improve conditions so that internal Communist pressures would be reduced. The means contemplated at the outset of 1950 as offering a prospect of success was the Marshall Plan method. The commitment to give arms to the Bao Dai government showed the same tendency in policy development, however, as that which had already taken place in Europe.

The answer to this and some of the other questions was, as already stated, given in the form of the immediate response to the invasion of Southern Korea. Without a formal commitment, and with respect to a country at least partially written off in advance as not readily defensible from the military standpoint, the moral and political requirements of the situation brought about the military response and showed a previously unavowed, and probably not yet consciously formulated, determination to use the necessary means to attain the declared objective of containing Soviet power at least within the limits to which it had been extended. The position was defined not merely for Korea but for the entire area when the Presidential order to lend the necessary military assistance to Korea included fleet dispositions to prevent a Communist attack on Formosa (while requesting the cessation of attacks from Formosa on continental China), and directing an increase in the defense establishment in the Philippines, together with a reexamination of the situation there with a view to rapid economic and political stabilization.

7. Communist China's Intervention in Korea

The major developments in the Far Eastern situation after the North Korean invasion of South Korea may be briefly summarized. As pointed out above (pp. 65-66), the initial attack brought about Security Council action calling for the immediate cessation of hostilities (a cease-fire) and the withdrawal of the North Korean forces to above the 38th parallel. The member states were requested "to render every assistance to the United Nations in the execution of this resolution and to refrain from giving assistance to the North Korean authorities." A resolution introduced by the United States on June 27, 1950, providing that the Security Council recommend that the member states should "furnish such assistance to the Republic of Korea as may be necessary to repel the armed attack and to restore international peace and security in the area," was adopted by seven votes, a bare majority. A resolution of July 7 instituted a unified command under the United States, which was requested to designate the commander. President Truman thereupon appointed General of the Army Douglas MacArthur to be Commanding General of the United Nations forces in Korea, leaving him concurrently Supreme Commander for the Allied Powers in Japan and Commander-in-Chief of United States forces in the Far East.

The return of the Soviet representative to the Security Council on August 1, to assume its presidency during that month, precluded further Security Council action, although the resolutions previously adopted were held to remain in force. After a Soviet veto on September 6 of an American resolution, the question was taken to the General Assembly, which on October 7 adopted a resolution based upon its resolutions of November 14, 1947, December 12, 1948, and October 21, 1949, and on the report of the United Nations Commission on Korea.

(a) A New Objective—Unification of Korea

In this resolution the General Assembly recalled "that there has been established a lawful government (the Government of the Republic of Korea) having effective jurisdiction over that part of Korea where the United Nations Temporary Commission on Korea was able to observe and consult . . . and that this is the only such government in Korea." It also recalled "that the essential objective of the resolutions of the General Assembly referred to was the establishment of a unified, independent and democratic government of Korea." Therefore, the resolution of October 7 recommended:

"(A) That all appropriate steps be taken to ensure conditions of stability throughout Korea.

"(B) That all constituent acts be taken, including the holding of elections, under the auspices of the United Nations *for the establishment of a unified, independent and democratic government in the sovereign state of Korea.* [Author's italics.]

"(C) That all sections and representative bodies of the population of Korea, South and North, be invited to cooperate with the organs of the United Nations in the restoration of peace, in the holding of elections and in the establishment of a unified government. . . .

"(D) That United Nations forces should not remain in any part of Korea otherwise than so far

as necessary for achieving the objectives specified
at (A) and (B) above;

"(E) That all necessary measures be taken to
accomplish the economic rehabilitation of Korea."

By this time the military situation had changed; there had
been a sufficient build-up of the United Nations forces to
enable them to assume the offensive. This had a bearing on
the changing of the objective from cessation of hostilities and
retirement of the North Korean forces to the 38th parallel,
to the "essential objective" of the earlier resolutions of the
General Assembly, namely, "the establishment of a unified,
independent and democratic government of Korea." The
Assembly resolution of October 7, it will be noted, con-
sistently referred to Korea, rather than to South Korea. Its
terminology as well as its terms, consequently, led readily
to the interpretation put on it by the United States and by the
Unified Command that it at least tacitly established unification
as the objective, and that it consequently authorized the extension of military operations to the Manchurian border of
Korea.

The military situation also seemed to put the only government recognized by the United States and the United Nations
in a position to extend its effective jurisdiction north of the
38th parallel, thus uniting Korea under its authority. Moves
taken along this line by the government of the Republic of
Korea, however, were checked by the Interim Committee,
which,

"Recalling that the Government of the Republic
of Korea has been recognized by the United Nations as a lawful government having effective control over that part of Korea where the United
Nations Temporary Commission on Korea was able
to observe and consult, and that there is conse-

quently no government that is recognized by the
United Nations as having legal and effective control over other parts of Korea; advises the Unified
Command to assume provisionally all responsibilities for the government and civil administration
of these parts of Korea which had not been recognized by the United Nations as being under the
effective control of the Government of Korea at the
out-break of hostilities, and which may now come
under occupation of United Nations forces. . . ."

Thus the objective of unification was not identified with
unification under the recognized government. Its attainment,
following successful military operations, would follow United
Nations supervision of the organization of North Korea
under a provisional democratic regime.

The nature of the problem, however, was again changed
when the Chinese Communist government intervened in behalf of the North Korean regime. This military intervention
had apparently not been expected, in spite of intelligence
reports of increasing concentrations of Chinese troops in
Manchuria and on the Korean border, and an intensification
of the "hate America" campaign in China proper. It was
apparently assumed that these developments had significance
only in relation to protection of the Manchurian frontier and
of Chinese interests in the power installations in northern
Korea close to the border, and possibly to strengthening the
Chinese Communist position against that of Russia in Manchuria itself. As to the intelligence on movement of Chinese
troops into Korea, in reply to a question by Senator Russell,
Chairman of the Joint Senate Committee, General Mac-
Arthur said:

"We had knowledge that the Chinese Communists had collected large forces along the Yalu

River. My own reconnaissance, you understand, was limited entirely to Korea; but the general information which was available, from China and other places, indicated large accumulations of troops.

"The Red Chinese, at that time, were putting out, almost daily, statements that they were not intervening, that these were volunteers only.

"About the middle of September our Secretary of State announced that he thought there was little chance, and no logic, in Chinese intervention.

"In November, our Central Intelligence Agency, here, had said that they felt there was little chance of any major intervention on the part of the Chinese forces.

"Now we, ourselves, on the front, realized that the North Korean forces were being stiffened, and our intelligence, made just before General Walker launched his attacks, indicated they thought from 40,000 to 60,000 men might be down there.

"Now you must understand that the intelligence that a nation is going to launch war, is not an intelligence that is available to a commander, limited to a small area of combat.

"That intelligence should have been given to me."[52]

On the same question General Bradley testified that: "We had the information that they had that capability and we always had the thought that they might enter it [the war], but we did not have any intelligence to the positive effect that they were going to intervene."[53] Consequently, it was not until the Chinese armies mounted a large-scale offensive against the United Nations forces, successfully driving them south of the 38th parallel, that the intervention of China was accepted as a fact of primary importance. China and the Peiping regime then became the focal point of policy even in relation to the Korean war.

An initial reaction in the United States, as elsewhere, was toward either an immediate or an ultimate writing-off of the Korean war as an unsuccessful experiment in the attempt to establish peace and security through international action. It was urged by Herbert Hoover and others that United States and United Nations forces should be immediately withdrawn from Korea to Japan, and thus conserved for future use. As an alternative, it was urged that they should not be reinforced, but that existing forces should fight delaying actions, accepting the probability that superior Chinese manpower would finally drive them from the peninsula. The January 12, 1951 directive from the Joint Chiefs of Staff to General MacArthur, as paraphrased by General Bradley, revealed the conclusion "that it is infeasible under existing conditions, including sustained major effort by Communist China, to hold the position in Korea for a protracted period."[54] Consequently, MacArthur was directed to defend in successive positions if necessary, and always with the understanding that the security of his troops was paramount.

Neither of these alternatives had to be acted upon. The relatively rapid containment of the Chinese offensive and the subsequent success of the limited but continuous counter-offensive of the United Nations forces, which by April 1951 had brought them again beyond the 38th parallel, once more changed the frame of reference for the development of policy.

While the military tide thus ebbed and flowed from the middle of November 1950 to the middle of May 1951, attempts were concurrently being made to find a political solution for the problems posed by the Chinese intervention in Korea. The first problem was that of bringing the military intervention to an end. Under Indian leadership, thirteen

Asian and Arab states introduced in the General Assembly a resolution, the adoption of which on December 14, 1950 led to the formation of a committee of three composed of the President of the Assembly (the head of the Iranian delegation, Nasrollah Entezam), L. B. Pearson, for Canada, and the Indian delegate, Sir Benegal N. Rau. This committee was "to determine the basis on which a satisfactory cease-fire in Korea can be arranged and to make recommendations to the General Assembly as soon as possible." The committee drafted proposals which it found itself unable to discuss directly with the Chinese People's Government, even though its envoy, General Wu, was still in New York.

In effect, the Chinese refused to discuss proposals for a cease-fire in Korea except in connection with other Far Eastern political issues still outstanding. Russia and China were apparently ready to define the conditions of a cease-fire in Korea only: (1) after the withdrawal of all foreign troops (apparently not initially including Chinese troops labeled "volunteers"); (2) after the seating of Chinese Communist delegates in the United Nations; (3) following the ending of the American "intervention" in support of the National Government in Formosa; and (4) in connection with the negotiation of a general Far Eastern settlement, including a treaty with Japan acceptable to Communist China and the Soviet Union. Under these circumstances it proved to be impossible to negotiate a cease-fire. The United States was willing to consider the proposals of the committee of three but not to accept the Chinese and Russian conditions, which represented a prejudgment of all the questions at issue between itself and China.

With the failure of the attempt to bring about an immediate cease-fire in Korea, the United States urged the adoption of a resolution formally finding the Peiping regime guilty of aggression. Such a step was finally taken on February 1,

1951. In addition to the finding of aggression, the resolution called upon the Central People's Government to cease hostilities in Korea and reaffirmed "the determination of the United Nations to continue its action in Korea to meet the aggression." A special committee of the General Assembly was formed to examine the problem and report on what additional measures might be necessary to solve it, besides those already authorized and taken by the member states.

The groundwork for this action had been laid in proposals made by the United States to the United Nations General Assembly in September 1950, with a view to preparing the way for action by the Assembly in other situations where the Security Council was unable to function. These proposals, somewhat modified, were embodied in what came to be called the "Uniting for Peace" resolution adopted on November 3, with the states in the Soviet bloc voting against it and India and Argentina abstaining. It was under the terms of this resolution that the Assembly proceeded to deal with the Chinese intervention in Korea, finally adopting the resolution labeling China an aggressor.

The hesitation of the United Nations in reaching that conclusion was apparently due to fear on the part of India and other states that such action would cut off what they perceived as a possibility of ending the war in Korea by negotiation, and also to fear that the United States would press for action which would enlarge the theater of military operations to include China itself. In addition, those states which had previously recognized the People's Government, notably India, apparently believed that no action should be taken with respect to China unless and until the Peiping regime had been given China's seat in the United Nations, so that it could participate in all discussions which involved it.

Thus, one of the questions which produced division among the states outside the Soviet bloc was that of recognition. On this issue the United States policy remained unchanged. It continued its support of the National Government as having the right to represent China. Its position against the transfer of the seat to the Communists was given additional support as the regime seeking admission to the United Nations launched an attack outside its territories against United Nations as well as United States forces. The February 1 resolution that the Chinese Communist government was engaged in aggression seemed to preclude recognizing it even for purposes of representation in the United Nations until the aggression was ended, either by the enforced retirement of Chinese troops from Korea or by the establishment of a cease-fire negotiated on the basis of their retirement north of the 38th parallel.

There remained, however, the possibility of an "additional measure" in the form of a recommendation to member states that they sever diplomatic relations with the Peiping regime. This would not affect those states which had not recognized it, nor would it be accepted by the states in the Soviet bloc, which had dissociated themselves from all forms of United Nations action on Korea on the ground of their legal invalidity. But it would call on Burma, Britain, India, and other states outside the Soviet bloc which had recognized the Peiping regime before the Korean aggression occurred to reverse their judgment. This reversal would be especially difficult for India to make because of its government's constantly reiterated view: (1) that the Central People's Government expressed the will and desires of the Chinese people, and that non-recognition in the form of severance of diplomatic relations consequently represented intervention in the domestic affairs of China; and (2) that the Chinese intervention in Korea was precipitated by Chinese Communist fear of attacks on their territory based on either Korea or Formosa.

(b) The Issue of Recognition

The first point, entirely divorced from the question of present aggression, is the important one. The American policy of non-recognition has been advertised by the Communists as indicative of an unwillingness to accept the results of civil war when they bring into power a regime viewed by the United States as unacceptable because of its economic and social policy or philosophy. This has led to the view of American recognition policy as "interventionist" and thus "imperialistic" because designed to take from the people of a country such as China the right to determine for themselves their form of government. This view is derived, however, from the negative expression of United States policy rather than from an appraisal of the facts on which American policy has been based. It also indicates an underlying suspicion of American motives and ultimate intentions.

Thus, American policy-makers are caught in the dilemma of the suspicion abroad that the United States seeks to overthrow the Communist regime in China and replace it with the Nationalist regime, and the domestic charge that it seeks to throw the Nationalists overboard and deal with the Communists.

The policy actually followed until the Chinese intervention in Korea seems to have been one of deferring recognition until the civil war in China had been concluded and until the *de facto* government, whether Communist or non-Communist, was able and willing to accept and discharge its international responsibilities and to enter into normal diplomatic relations with the United States.* From this latter point of view, the circumstances of the Chinese aggression in Korea

---

*This was written before the controversy in October 1951 over Harold E. Stassen's contention that the State Department had "considered" recognition.—ED.

served to underscore the soundness of the policy of deferring recognition. In the argument over American policy toward the Peiping regime, the Communists have concentrated on the question of Formosa. But the real issue, as suggested above, was much more fundamental. The larger issues were drawn together in the question of the method of ending the Korean war and the Chinese aggression in Korea.

The problem of recognition actually of course has two distinct aspects. The one just summarized from the standpoint of American policy is that of defining the conditions on which a state or government is willing to enter directly into political relations with a new government or state. The other is the problem of transfer of a seat and voting rights in the United Nations from one government to another. The China case poses a special problem within this aspect of the general problem because of China's permanent representation, with the so-called veto, on the Security Council. The question of the veto is involved also from the point of view of American policy because of the position of the United States as a permanent member of the Security Council. On this side of the question, the policy of the United States had apparently been defined, as suggested above, as that of opposition to replacing the Nationalist delegates with representatives of the Communist regime, but of acquiescence in whatever conclusions were registered by the stipulated majority in various United Nations organs. In other words, in the Security Council, such questions having been previously defined by the United States as procedural, it was apparently not American policy to exercise the veto if that were necessary to keep the Chinese Communists out of the United Nations.

In describing American policy Secretary Acheson said:

> "we had opposed the entrance of the Chinese Communists into the United Nations, and we had opposed it, I thought, very successfully. The attitude

of the Government, it has been, I think, clear, was expressed by General Marshall that we cannot allow governments that want to get into the United Nations to shoot their way in. . . .

"There are 46 organizations of the United Nations and its affiliated special agencies to which the Chinese might be admitted if that action was taken by these bodies. The question has come up 77 times in these various 46 bodies. The vote has been against the admission 76 times out of the 77."[55]

American policy of not admitting the Communists, it may thus be said, has been implemented through the majority process. It has not, therefore, been necessary as yet actually to approach the question in terms of exercise or non-exercise of the veto. If, however, there should be a majority in favor of seating the Chinese Communists in the immediate future, it became less certain than it appeared to be in 1950 that the United States would view the issue as procedural and thus not subject to the veto. General Marshall indicated the view of the Defense Department to be that the veto should be used if necessary and if legally possible. Secretary Acheson, in reply to questions as to policy on the veto, stated:

"If we are in a minority, then the point arises as to what to do about that situation. I should think before that arose, and if one believed that that situation was going to arise, the thing to do would be to ask the World Court what the significance of a vote of a permanent member on this matter is.

"If the World Court would decide that that is a veto, then that settles the matter in the Security Council. You have to get some decision of that sort because if you are in a minority of four or less on the main question, you will be in a minority of

four or less on the subsidiary question of whether
this is or isn't, whether an adverse vote is or isn't,
a veto."[56]

This somewhat modified the earlier position as defined
by Senator Warren R. Austin, the United States representative
on the Security Council, that "We believe in rule by law and
we believe the law does not give us the power to veto in this
matter."[57] Pressure from Congressmen, as well as pressure
of events, had modified the previous certainty as to the un-
lawfulness of the veto, but the United States was now willing
to accept a judgment made by the Permanent Court on the
question.

As pointed out above, the Peiping regime made it clear that
it would not agree to withdraw its troops from Korea except
on its own terms. Those terms the United States was not willing to accept. Nor was the United States willing to negotiate
on questions at issue, other than the terms of a cease-fire in
Korea, until the Chinese aggression against the United Nations had been ended. But in spite of the adoption of the
resolution labeling China an aggressor, it was clear that it
would be difficult to secure an authorization from the United
Nations to carry the war to China. It had been, in fact, fear
that the United States would press for the adoption of "additional measures" of a military nature, as well as the continued
belief among the Asian nations in the possibility of a negotiated settlement, which made it difficult for the United
States quickly to secure the adoption of a resolution which
actually embodied only a formal declaration of the established
fact of aggression. European states were afraid that a chain
of events would be started which would ultimately bring
about such commitment of American power against China
as to weaken seriously the common defense against the Soviet
Union in Europe and the Middle East.

(c) The Relief of General MacArthur

An initial action against China directly related to the conduct of military operations in Korea would have been the bombing of the bases in Manchuria from which the Chinese armies operated. Suggestions to this effect came recurrently from United Nations Headquarters in Tokyo in connection with reports on the military aspects of the situation following the Chinese intervention. Without authorization to extend air operations to Manchuria, it was held that the war could only go into a prolonged stalemate which would have to be ended by political means. The American government, however, did not press for such an authorization from the United Nations, possibly because it did not anticipate sufficient support readily to command the necessary two-thirds majority, but more probably because it also thought in terms of a chain of events which might precipitate the war with the Soviet Union which it sought to postpone or avoid.

That there was conflict of opinion within the United States over Far Eastern policy had been revealed in Congressional debates as well as in the press of the country. General MacArthur's views on many of the questions at issue had been introduced into this debate before his return to the United States. His views with respect to policy toward Japan and with respect to the problem of an early peace treaty were well known, and had substantially affected American policy. On the more politically explosive question of Formosa his views had been made known and publicly argued, although the President caused his message to the Veterans of Foreign Wars in August 1950 to be withdrawn. Subsequently, at the Wake Island conference of October 15, the President and General MacArthur announced that they were in agreement on major issues.

At this conference, according to *The New York Times,*

"General MacArthur indicated he would conform with the policies laid down in Washington. After that General MacArthur invited the enemy commander to negotiate with him in the field, though he knew that the United Nations itself was trying to lay the groundwork for negotiations looking toward the end of the fighting. Finally came his letter to Representative Joseph W. Martin Jr. of Massachusetts, that struck at the very foundation of the Administration's grand strategy, which the Joint Chiefs of Staff had a major role in planing."[58]

Following this, on April 11, 1951, General MacArthur was removed from all of his commands. He thereupon returned to the United States under circumstances which reopened on a grand scale debate on United States Far Eastern policy.

Although it was given only incidental exposition in his address before Congress on April 19,[59] a basic difference of opinion existed between General MacArthur and the Departments of State and Defense over the relative importance to the United States of Western Europe and Eastern Asia. During World War II, General MacArthur had reluctantly acquiesced, but had never concurred, in the decision of the Joint Chiefs of Staff to give the war against Germany priority over the war against Japan. And he did not apparently concur in the present view that Western Europe should be listed first in order of priority for purposes of containment of Soviet expansionism. In his address he started with the same premise as that on which government policy had been based, that "The issues are global, and so interlocked that to consider the problems of one sector oblivious to those of another is but to court disaster for the whole." But in the following sentences he presented a different emphasis from Washington's:

"While Asia is commonly referred to as the gateway to Europe, it is no less true that Europe is the gateway to Asia, and the broad influence of the one cannot fail to have its impact on the other. There are those who claim our strength is inadequate to protect on both fronts, that we cannot divide our effort. I can think of no greater expression of defeatism. If a potential enemy can divide his strength on two fronts, it is for us to counter his effort. The Communist threat is a global one. Its successful advance in one sector threatens the destruction of every other sector. You cannot appease or otherwise surrender to Communism in Asia without simultaneously undermining our efforts to halt its advance in Europe."

The contrasting official point of view was presented by General Bradley, Chairman of the Joint Chiefs of Staff, as follows:

"From a global viewpoint—and with the security of our Nation of prime importance—our military mission is to support a policy of preventing communism from gaining the manpower, the resources, the raw materials, and the industrial capacity essential to world domination. If Soviet Russia ever controls the entire Eurasian land mass, then the Soviet-satellite imperialism may have the broad base upon which to build the military power to rule the world. . . . Korea, in spite of the importance of the engagement, must be looked upon with proper perspective."[60]

While the implications of this difference in emphasis can be considered fairly only as part of an analysis of the specific proposals which General MacArthur advanced for action to win a decision in the Korean war, it must be noted here that they involve judgment as to the effect of such action on the policies of the Soviet Union. The official conclusion has been that the enlargement of the theater of active war to include Chinese territories in order to win a decisive victory in Korea would invite direct retaliation by the Soviet Union, which might take the form of Soviet military action in Western Europe at a time when American military power was heavily committed in China. The consequence, it is argued, might well be the loss of the area of primary importance to the United States.

As General Bradley put it: "Red China is not the powerful nation seeking to dominate the world. Frankly, in the opinion of the Joint Chiefs of Staff, this strategy would involve us in the wrong war, at the wrong place, at the wrong time, and with the wrong enemy."[61] General Marshall's statement of the difference of viewpoint is even more direct:

> "He [General MacArthur] would have us accept the risk [of] involvement not only in an extension of the war with Red China, but in an all-out war with the Soviet Union. He would have us do this even at the expense of losing our allies and wrecking the coalition of free peoples throughout the world. He would have us do this even though the effect of such action might expose Western Europe to attack by the millions of Soviet troops poised in Middle and Eastern Europe."[62]

This conclusion, however, would seem to be rejected by General MacArthur:

> "Why, my soldiers asked of me, surrender military advantages to an enemy in the field? I could not answer. Some may say to avoid spread of the

conflict into an all-out war with China. Others, to avoid Soviet intervention. Neither explanation seems valid, for China is already engaging with the maximum power it can commit, and the Soviet will not necessarily mesh its actions with our moves. Like a cobra, any new enemy will more likely strike whenever it feels that the relativity in military or other potential is in its favor on a world-wide basis."

While the language is not altogether clear, the conclusion apparently was that action against China along the lines proposed (a) would not lead to an overcommitment of the United States in the Far East, and (b) would not lead to Soviet intervention in Europe unless the Kremlin felt that it had a world preponderance of power.

The specific proposals advanced by General MacArthur in his address to Congress which, if adopted, would involve change or modification of established policy, were formulated, he said, to meet the requirements of a

"new war and an entirely new situation, a situation not contemplated when our forces were committed against the North Korean invaders; a situation which called for new decisions in the diplomatic sphere to permit the realistic adjustment of military strategy. This new war resulted from Chinese Communist military intervention in force in Korea. While no man in his right mind would advocate sending our ground forces into continental China, and such was never given a thought, the new situation did urgently demand a drastic revision of strategic planning if our political aim was to defeat this new enemy as we had defeated the old. Apart from the military need, as I saw it, to neutralize the sanctuary protection given the enemy north of the

Yalu, I felt that military necessity in the conduct of the war made necessary (1) The intensification of our economic blockade against China. (2) The imposition of a naval blockade against the China coast. (3) Removal of restrictions on air reconnaissance of China's coastal area and of Manchuria. (4) Removal of restrictions on the forces of the Republic of China on Formosa, with logistical support to contribute to their effective operation against the common enemy."[62a]

In advancing these specific proposals General MacArthur said that "from a military standpoint the above views have been fully shared in the past by practically every military leader concerned with the Korean compaign, including our own joint chiefs of staff." (The subsequent testimony of Secretary Marshall and Generals Bradley and Collins did not altogether agree with that of General MacArthur on this point; Generals Bradley and Collins in particular expressed disagreement with General MacArthur's military views.) And it was on the basis of military considerations that he said that "I have constantly called for the new political decisions essential to a solution." But political decisions necessarily had to be based upon broad political considerations, as well as on military considerations. It was the underlying political considerations involved in or resulting from specific military decisions which actually were under national debate as a result of General MacArthur's return to the United States and his campaign for a change of policy.

Without military action against China outside of Korea, MacArthur held that a victory in Korea could not be won; that the best that could be hoped for was a prolonged stalemate. "War's very object," he told the Congress, "is victory, not prolonged indecision. In war there can be no substitute for victory." The administration apparently held, on the other hand, that localizing the military operations in Korea and preventing there a successful aggression, if that could be done, would represent the attainment of its objectives, and thus victory, since it sought to prevent the expansion of Communist power and to avoid precipitating World War III.[63] If the Soviet Union should precipitate World War III, a further American objective would be to have in readiness a strong coalition of powers capable of winning a victory in that war. The administration was not prepared, consequently, to take action beyond that authorized by the United Nations if it were clear that such action would disrupt the anti-Soviet coalition.

The British as well as the Indian government (both of which had recognized the Peiping government before the outbreak of the Korean war) had expressed strong opposition to any extension of military operations to China. This indicated a probability that any such extension of the theater of operations might have the consequence of ending even the Korean war as a coalition or United Nations undertaking. This would not materially change the situation in Korea in terms of military power. But it would raise questions as to the conditions of continued effective Anglo-American cooperation in Europe and the Middle East and concerning the further development of the North Atlantic Treaty Organization.[64]

What would be the general global effects of a breakdown of the anti-Soviet coalition in the Far East cannot of course be stated. It has certainly been assumed by the American government, however, that such a development in the Far East would have seriously weakening effects elsewhere. The conclusion has been drawn in Europe as well as in Washington that joint European defense against a possible Soviet attack would be weakened because of an increasing commitment of American forces in the Far East with a view to winning a military decision over China. From the point of view of global strategy, in other words, an important consideration to be weighed against others has been whether, and the extent to which, the global coalition would be weakened or disrupted by taking the specific actions proposed.

The question thus became whether, from the standpoint of global strategy, the immediate military advantages would be sufficiently great to compensate for the immediate and the longer-run political and possibly military disadvantages. These all related to the probable effects of the proposed actions on the Soviet Union as well as on China. Against the established policy of making the necessary adjustments to ensure the maintenance of the coalition, General MacArthur advanced the view that these broader considerations should be disregarded and that we should, if necessary, go it alone in the Far East.

Neutralization of "the sanctuary protection given the enemy north of the Yalu," which was advocated by General MacArthur in his address to Congress and in his testimony before the Joint Committee, must be taken to mean at least the bombing of Chinese air bases and troop concentrations in Manchuria. The purpose of bombing air bases would be to destroy on the ground the reported accumulations of planes which might at any moment be thrown decisively into the Chinese military operations in Korea. Such bombing would have direct relevance to the success or failure of United Nations military operations in Korea. But if the action were taken in anticipation of extensive use of air power by the Chinese in Korea, rather than after such use, the action might invite reprisals by the Chinese against Japan, which the Chinese have begun to label the "American sanctuary," where American air power has been based. It might also call into play the Sino-Soviet alliance.

Both of these were asserted as reasonable possibilities and not necessarily as probabilities. As such, nevertheless, they had to be considered by those charged with the determination of policy. Such critics of existing policy as General MacArthur discounted, from the point of view of probability, such an extension of Chinese action on the ground that Chinese power was completely committed in Korea. It was apparently also their view that the probability would be against direct and large-scale Soviet assistance to China resulting from the bombing of Manchurian installations. But, to the limited extent that there was such a possibility of Soviet intervention, they held that this should not deter the United States from taking action which would reduce immediately the casualty lists in Korea.

The proposal made by General MacArthur that there be "Removal of restrictions on air reconnaissance of China's coastal areas and of Manchuria" must be viewed in relation to his general argument. It must therefore be concluded that air operations designed to develop intelligence as to enemy troop concentrations and dispositions, base facilities, location of arsenals, and supply lines, were not the real proposal. "Air reconnaissance" would not bring about the destruction of "the enemy built-up bases north of the Yalu." In other words, the proposal if adopted would undoubtedly have led to strategic bombing with a view to compelling the Chinese to withdraw their forces from Korea and accept defeat there.

The proposals for the intensification of the economic blockade against China and the imposition of a naval blockade against the China coast were, in effect, proposals of full economic sanctions against China, again with a view to so weakening Peiping as to bring about military capitulation in Korea. The principal question raised by such proposals is that of effectiveness in relation to the objective. The effectiveness of economic sanctions varies (1) in terms of the nature and stage of development of the economy of the country to which they are applied, and (2) with the completeness with which that country can be cut off from outside supply of essential materials. As to the first proposition, it is apparent that the Chinese economy has not yet been sufficiently developed, from the point of view of economic specialization and industrialization, to be as seriously and as immediately affected by boycott and blockade measures as would be the case if such measures were directed against a developed and industrialized state. As to the second proposition, in view of Russia's long land frontier with China, the boycott and blockade would be incomplete and might consequently lose much of its effectiveness. If otherwise complete it would be effective, in other words, only with respect to essential commodities which could not be supplied by or by way of the Soviet Union. (General MacArthur held, however, that inadequate and vulnerable transportation facilities between China and Russia would limit severely the possibilities of shipment.)

In any event, and under the best of circumstances, economic sanctions yield results by the slow process of attrition. Consequently, if primary reliance were put on them, it would have to be assumed that they would not have a quick and decisive effect on operations in Korea. This would have to be anticipated to avoid immediate demands for action of a more far-reaching military character designed to produce immediate results. Otherwise economic sanctions would have to be evaluated not merely from the standpoint of their effectiveness, but also as part of a possible chain of events culminating ultimately in World War III. By themselves, because of their lack of maximum effectiveness against a country at China's stage of development and with its geopolitical relationship to the Soviet Union, and their inability to produce immediately decisive results, boycott and blockade could certainly be viewed as measures which would not precipitate application of the alliance between Communist China and the Soviet Union, and thus lead to World War III. For that reason they had been most emphasized among the "additional measures" proposed for consideration even before General MacArthur was relieved of his command responsibilities. The hesitancy in pressing for their adoption would seem to have been (a) because of the view that, for the reason suggested above, they cannot be dissociated from the question of additional military measures necessary to produce the desired result of Chinese capitulation in Korea, and (b) because of British reluctance to cut off all trade with China via Hongkong. It should be noted, however, that one such "additional measure" was approved by the United Nations General Assembly on May 18, when it adopted by a vote of 47-0 a United States proposal for an embargo on shipment of arms and certain other strategic materials to Communist China and North Korea. This was a recommendation to the member states, which the states in the Soviet bloc certainly would not put into effect. There was some question also as to how it would be operative in the cases of India, Burma, and Indonesia.

(d) The Problem of Formosa

From the point of view of American policy, General MacArthur's proposals for blockade and bombing of China were not of primary importance in the controversy between the administration and its critics. His proposal for "removal of restrictions on the forces of the Republic of China on Formosa, with logistical support to contribute to their effective operation," whether or not with a view to their use against the mainland, on the other hand, cut directly to the heart of the conflict of postwar opinion on Far Eastern policy. In the public debate the two distinct aspects of the question have not been separately considered. This has resulted in considerable confusion of claim and counter-claim.

The first aspect of the question involves Formosa itself in relation to China and in relation to the outer perimeter of the

American security zone. Formosa was originally transferred from China to Japan under the treaty terminating the first Sino-Japanese war of 1894-1895, and its restoration to China was defined as a war objective by the Cairo Declaration. Chinese administration under the National Government was instituted following VJ Day. After the Kuomintang military collapse on the mainland, the seat of the National Government was transferred to Formosa and the remnants of Chiang's armies were evacuated to the island. From Formosa as a base, organized opposition to Communist rule of China has been continued under what, for the United States and many other states, continued to be the recognized government of China.

It is this control of Formosa which has given the principal support to the National Government's claim to continued recognition and to China's seat in the Security Council and other United Nations organs. But it has made this claim as the government of China and not as the government of Formosa, since both the Nationalists and the Chinese Communists demand fulfillment of the terms of the Cairo Declaration. Thus, neither has been responsive to the view that title to the island has not passed from Japan to China until there has been a formal cession in a treaty of peace with Japan.[65] Such responsiveness might be shown by the National Government if it should become clear that Formosa's detachment from China was the only alternative to its incorporation into Communist-ruled China. Such a choice would have to be made, however, only when the Communists had the freedom of action and the power to undertake a successful invasion of Formosa. And at that point the United States, as well as the National Government, would have to decide whether or not to acquiesce in Communist control of the island and thus in the completion of the destruction of Kuomintang power by the Chinese Communists in all of China.

In the first months of 1950, the generally accepted view of policy as defined by the Department of State was that of acquiescence in Communist control of Formosa, if the Communists were able to take it from the Nationalists. The ability of the National Government to maintain itself on Formosa against a Communist invasion was discounted on the ground that the defense would be conducted by the same government that Secretary Acheson held to have been thoroughly discredited in China because of its inefficiency, corruption, and military ineptitude; and by the troops which had been defeated by the Communists on the mainland partly because of their low morale and lack of will to fight, and partly because of the incompetence of their leadership. The misrule of the Kuomintang on Formosa in the immediate postwar years, it was further argued, would weaken the military defense of the island through active subversion by those who had suffered from Kuomintang misrule and through a general reluctance on the part of the population of the island vigorously to support the defense. A forecast of what would happen in the event of invasion was held to have been given in the ease with which Hainan island had been successfully invaded.

Thus, if the civil war were extended to Formosa, an outcome favorable to the Communists was anticipated.[66] Viewing the question, until the Korean war, as a projection of an internal conflict, the State Department, not being prepared to accept the onus of intervening in the internal struggle in behalf of the "discredited" Nationalists, was prepared to acquiesce in the extension of Communist control to Formosa, and probably, as a result, to accept the transfer of the seat of China in the United Nations to the Peiping government. The way had been paved for this by declaration of intent not to exercise the veto. (See above, pp. 56, 108-109).

In his message of August 1950 to the Veterans of Foreign Wars (withdrawn by presidential order), General Mac-

Arthur intended publicly to register a dissent to this policy on strategic grounds. He argued then, as he did subsequently, that Formosa had such importance to the maintenance of the outer island perimeter security zone of the United States, anchored on Japan in the north and the Philippines in the south, that it must not be allowed to fall into the hands of any state hostile to the United States. In this he seems also to have expressed the view of the Joint Chiefs of Staff.

When the North Korean attack was launched in June 1950, the United States unilaterally declared the neutralization of Formosa for the period of the military operations in Korea. The Nationalists were instructed to refrain from air and other operations against the mainland and the Communists were debarred from an invasion of Formosa. The Seventh Fleet was ordered to enforce these prohibitions. This action, although announced as designed to localize military operations in Korea, also settled the conflict of policy by acceptance of the military thesis that considerations of national security required that Formosa should be kept out of the hands of the anti-American Communist government of China, at least during the period of military operations in Korea.[67]

If that government should cease its aggression in Korea; if it should be recognized by the United States; and if normal relations between the two governments should thereafter be established, then present American policy with respect to Formosa would have to be reexamined. We should have to determine whether we would support or acquiesce (1) in implementation of the Cairo Declaration against the National Government, viewed as the government of Formosa only, or (2) whether we would support a solution which would detach Formosa from China. Meanwhile, however, the question at issue has become that of the relationship of the Nationalist armies to the Korean war.

The first decision on that question was not to accept an

offer made by Chiang of a contingent of troops to be used in Korea as part of the United Nations force. The primary Nationalist responsibility, it was held, was to defend Formosa. There was apparently some initial doubt as to its ability to discharge that responsibility without assistance. This doubt led to a request from the Joint Chiefs of Staff that General MacArthur send a military mission from his headquarters "to Formosa, to go over the command there, air, sea and ground, in connection with the defense of Formosa against any Communist attack on that island." The mission returned to Tokyo late in August, and their report "had a great effect upon the opinion of the Chiefs of Staff in relation to the utilization of these particular troops."[68]

At this time General MacArthur concurred in the view of the Joint Chiefs of Staff that it would be inadvisable to utilize the Nationalist troops in the Korean war, but after the Chinese Communist intervention in Korea he changed his opinion. As he explained to the Senate committee, in the summer of 1950 Chinese Communist troops were massed on the mainland, in position to attack Formosa, and he therefore felt that Formosa's defenses should not be weakened. Later, however, after these Communist troops had been moved to Manchuria, removing the immediate threat to Formosa, MacArthur recommended that the Nationalist troops be "unleashed," in order to relieve the pressure on the UN forces in Korea.

As to the military effectiveness of the Nationalist troops, General MacArthur told the Senate committee:

> "The generalissimo has probably in the neighborhood of a half million troops. The personnel is excellent. . . . They have a good morale. Their material equipment is spotty. They lack artillery. They lack trucks. They lack a great many of the

modern refinements. They are capable of being made into a very excellent force. . . . I should say they probably have between 200 and 250 planes. Their pilots are rather good. And for such a jerk-water group, they make a pretty brave showing. Their navy is not a navy. It is a conglomeration of small ships. . . . My own estimate would be, after the material was there, that those troops would be in very good shape, probably as good as they ever could be made outside of combat, within 4 months."[69]

It was on the basis of this appraisal of the effectiveness of the regime and of its military forces that General MacArthur proposed the "removal of restrictions on the forces of the republic of China on Formosa, with logistical support to contribute to their effective operation against the common enemy." His appraisal was not accepted as correct by the American government, although it took measures to strengthen the Nationalist forces at least for defense. Arms shipments to Formosa were resumed late in 1950, and a military mission was sent in May 1951.

General MacArthur's view of the use of National Government troops on the mainland was that: "They could infiltrate into Indochina. They could go in small forays and come back or they could go to the mainland just exactly as they came to Formosa, in their own junks and so on. . . . Even as a threat they would have relieved the pressure on my command."[70]

Thus, he proposed essentially diversionary operations related to the Korean war and to the accomplishment of limited American and United Nations purposes rather than American logistical support of operations on the mainland designed to accomplish the purpose of the National Government. That

the Far East. This view was expressed as that of a theater commander without responsibility beyond his own theater. It was based, however, on his view that the risk of Soviet action was limited, and should be accepted by the United States. The testimony of Generals Marshall and Bradley indicated that the risk was much greater and more immediate in their opinion than General MacArthur conceded. And because of this threat the administration policy has been directed toward the maintenance of the coalition.

(e) *Steps Toward a Treaty with Japan*

The limitation which this imposed was clearly revealed in the attempts made to adjust United States policy toward Japan to the changed Far Eastern situation. It took laborious negotiations to bring other states to accept the American policy of revival of Japanese strength and of concluding a peace treaty which would permit the reemergence of Japan as a power factor in the Far Eastern and Pacific areas. Until the United States was prepared to commit itself to a defense pact which would be operative against Japan if it should again become an aggressor, fear of Japan prevented agreement among the states in the Western coalition on the terms of a Japanese peace treaty acceptable to them as well as to the United States.

The draft text of such a defense pact between the United States, Australia and New Zealand was finally initialed on July 12, 1951. One reason for restricting the number of participants was indicated in the preamble:

> "The United States already has arrangements pursuant to which its armed forces are stationed in the Philippines, and has armed forces and administrative responsibilities in the Ryukyus, and upon the coming into force of the Japanese peace treaty

> may also station armed forces in and about Japan
> to assist in the preservation of peace and security in
> the Japan area."[71]

This indicated that the problem of security for the Philippines was viewed as solved through a separate guarantee. Although Britain had indicated a desire to participate in the treaty, it presumably concluded that Australia and New Zealand might be expected to safeguard Commonwealth interests.

The nine articles of the Three-Power Treaty were obviously written with a view to organizing the problem of security in the Pacific within the framework of the United Nations system. The important additional security element in the treaty was the stipulation of Article 4, paragraph 1, that "Each party recognizes that an armed attack in the Pacific area on any of the parties would be dangerous to its own peace and safety and declares that it would act to meet the common danger in accordance with its constitutional processes."

With this additional guarantee of security, it was possible to assume sufficient agreement on the text of a treaty with Japan for the American Department of State to issue invitations to a conference at San Francisco for the purpose not of negotiating but of signing an agreed text of a peace treaty. Bilateral negotiations were meanwhile continued until it was possible for the United States and Britain to circulate a "final text" on August 16. This showed some modifications in the originally published draft, made to meet objections raised to some of its provisions. The most important change was designed to keep open the possibility of future reparations payments.

By August 27 thirty-nine of the invited states had notified the United States of their intention to send delegations to San Francisco, with eight additional probable acceptances;

India had declined. The accepting governments included the U.S.S.R., Poland, and Czechoslovakia. The Soviet purpose in accepting was not altogether clear since the U.S.S.R. had previously joined Communist China in denunciation of the treaty and the method of its negotiation. On this question of Soviet purposes Mr. Dulles, as reported in the *New York Times,* August 16, said: "We are not yet clear as to what this means. We hope that it does not mean that the Russians are sending a wrecking crew to try to demolish a structure of Japanese peace which has been built carefully and soundly until now it is complete save for the formal dedication." It was not, in other words, assumed that the Soviet delegates would have instructions merely to sign the treaty. It was, however, felt that without the signature of the Soviet participants, and over their objections if necessary, the treaty would be signed by a sufficient number of states to bring it into effect.*

The principal negotiator of the treaty, Ambassador John Foster Dulles, gave an overall characterization of its terms as follows: ". . . the proposed treaty does not put Japan under any permanent restrictions or disabilities which will make her different or less sovereign than any other free nation. The treaty will, in fact, restore Japan as a sovereign equal, and the treaty is truly one of reconciliation."

Despite this, the treaty does require Japan to accept the loss of the imperial territorial position established since the Meiji Restoration. Thus Japan, "recognizing the independence of Korea, renounces all right, title and claim to Korea, including the islands of Quelpart, Port Hamilton and Dagelet," but not Tsushima, to which the Korean government had ad-

---

*The treaty was signed on September 8 by Japan and 48 Allied nations, not including the Soviet Union. A security pact between the United States and the Philippines had been signed in Washington on August 30, and the three-power pact among Australia, New Zealand, and the United States, referred to above, was formally concluded at San Francisco on September 1.—ED.

vanced a claim. There is a similar renunciation with respect
to Formosa and the Pescadores, the Kurile Islands, and "that
portion of Saghalin and the islands adjacent to it over which
Japan acquired sovereignty as a consequence of the Treaty
of Portsmouth of September 5, 1905." Thus the ultimate title
to these territories is not established in the Japanese peace
treaty.

On the other hand, Japan not only "renounces all right,
title and claim in connection with the League of Nations
Mandate system" but it also "accepts the action of the United
Nations Security Council of April 2, 1947, extending the
trusteeship system to the Pacific Islands formerly under mandate to Japan." The renunciation here is specific and in favor
of the United States, which has a strategic trusteeship for these
islands.

With respect to the Ryukyus (of which Okinawa is one),

> "Japan will concur in any proposal of the United
> States to the United Nations to place under its
> trusteeship system, with the United States as the
> sole administering authority, the Ryukyu Islands
> south of 29 north latitude, the Nanpo Shoto south
> of Sofu Gan . . . and the Parece Vela and Marcus
> Island. Pending the making of such a proposal and
> affirmative action thereon, the United States will
> have the right to exercise all or any powers of ad-
> ministration, legislation, and jurisdiction over the
> territory and inhabitants of these islands, including
> their territorial waters."

These territorial losses register the verdict of the war, as
do such provisions of the draft treaty as the stipulations of
Article 11 with respect to war criminals and those of Article
10 with respect to special rights and interests in China.

Detailed analysis of the terms of the draft treaty is unnecessary here. It must be noted, however, that Chapter III, titled Security, registers the outcome of the final shift in American policy from the premise of Japan as an enemy power. Article 5 is designed to bring Japan as completely as possible within the United Nations security system. Article 6 carries the matter a long step further from the point of view of connection between the security problem of Japan and that of the United States. This article provides for withdrawal of all occupation forces from Japan "as soon as possible after the coming into force of the present treaty, and in any case not later than 90 days thereafter." It then stipulates that "nothing in this provision shall however prevent the stationing or retention of foreign armed forces in Japanese territory under or in consequence of any bilateral or multilateral agreements which have been or may be made between one or more of the Allied Powers, on the one hand, and Japan on the other."

Thus it may be anticipated that an agreement between the United States and Japan, giving the United States military rights in Japan, will be announced before the expiration of this 90-day period, unless there is a significant change in the international climate.* The treaty and such an agreement will have the effect together of terminating S.C.A.P. and eliminating its civilian activities while maintaining in Japan the American Far East Command headquarters.

(f) The Problem of Fostering Reform

Another real difficulty which must be overcome by the coalition against Soviet imperialism in eastern Asia and the Pacific lies in the continued existence in many of the countries concerned of economic, political, and social conditions which can be effectively exploited by insubstantial Communist minorities. Governmental and administrative reform,

---

*Such an agreement was signed in San Francisco on September 8.—ED.

such as is reported to have been instituted on Formosa, is essential if the full benefits of the policy of technical, financial, and economic assistance are to be realized. Recognition of this was shown in the recommendations of the Bell Mission to the Philippines. But pressure from the outside for political reform has had to be cautiously applied in countries which have newly emerged into independence or self-government in order to avoid the charge of imperialism which would stimulate a nationalist reaction against the state applying pressure. Such nationalist sentiment can readily be capitalized either by the governing elements to avoid change or by Communist elements to stimulate antagonism both to the government in power and to the United States.

The United States, to realize its objectives, finds itself necessarily compelled to respond to appeals for assistance from governments which it may not regard as altogether acceptable, and with whose policies it may be far from sympathetic. Otherwise it might have to acquiesce in the displacement of those governments because of their inability to improve economic conditions. The fact that has to be generally recognized is that assistance from the outside can be given to the people of a country only through the medium of their government. This fact presents a dilemma to the United States which it has not yet satisfactorily resolved, and this conditions agreement in national opinion on the development and application of programs of technical, financial, and economic aid in Asian lands as it has not in Western Europe.

(g) Securing a Stable Peace in the Far East

The cease-fire negotiations begun in July 1951 opened still another chapter in the tangled story of the Korean crisis. But even the cessation of hostilities could not, by itself, create the conditions for stable peace in the Far East. That would require a general agreement among all of the parties in interest in Korea (North Koreans, South Koreans, Chinese, Russians, Americans, as well as the United Nations) on the conditions of unification of the country. Nor can political stability and firm peace be expected until there has been a final and generally accepted decision, one way or the other, on the outcome of the Chinese civil war, which would make possible a solution of the problem of recognition and that of the status of Formosa.

The Korean crisis precipitated a long and bitter debate, which has not yet ended, over American policy in Asia. The fact is sometimes overlooked that this debate revealed areas of agreement within the United States, as well as the highly publicized areas of disagreement. The major cleavages have been over policy toward China, and over methods of terminating the Korean war. And even here the differences may have been less over fundamental questions of policy than over the question of who should exercise the power of decision in the establishment of policy within the United States.

Notes

1. Vera Micheles Dean, *Main Trends in Postwar American Foreign Policy*, American I.P.R., 1949, pp. 19-20.

2. *Ibid.*, p. 19.

3. Joseph C. Grew, *Ten Years in Japan*, Simon and Schuster, New York, 1944, p. 76.

4. Cordell Hull, *Memoirs*, MacMillan, New York, 1948, Vol. I, pp. 535-536.

5. *Ibid.*, p. 538.

6. H. M. Vinacke, *History of the Far East in Modern Times*, 5th ed., Crofts, New York, 1950, p. 602. Hereafter cited as Vinacke.

7. *Ibid.*, p. 605.

8. *United States Relations with China*, Dept. of State Pub. 3573, Far Eastern Series 30, 1949, p. 35. Hereafter cited as *China White Paper*, 1949.

9. *Ibid*, p. 36.

10. *Ibid.*, p. 37.

11. *Ibid.*, Annex 47, pp. 567-568.

12. John Davies, in *China White Paper*, 1949, pp. 566-567.

13. *China White Paper*, 1949, p. 89.

14. *Ibid.*, p. 92.

15. *Ibid.*, p. 469.

16. Vinacke, p. 642.

17. Congressman Mansfield, for example, reporting to Congress on his mission to China, stated: "On the basis of information which I have been able to gather, it appears to me that both the Communists and the Kuomintang are more interested in preserving their respective Parties at this time and have been for the past two years than they are in carrying on the war against Japan. Each Party is more interested in its own status because both feel that America will guarantee victory." (*China White Paper*, 1949, p. 61.)

18. Vinacke, p. 643.

19. *China White Paper*, 1949, Annex No. 39, pp. 530-531.

20. *Ibid.*, pp. 552-553.

21. *Ibid.*, p. 67.

22. *Ibid.*, p. 72.

23. *Ibid.*, p. 73.

24. *Ibid.*, pp. 74-75.

25. *Ibid.*, pp. 81-82.

26. *Ibid.*, p. 75.

27. *Ibid.*, pp. 311-312.

28. See paragraphs 6-9 of President Truman's Statement on United States Policy Toward China December 15, 1945. Text in *China White Paper*, 1949, pp. 607-608.

29. Sumner Welles, *Where Are We Heading?*, Harper, New York, 1946, p. 296.

30. It was estimated as of VJ Day that the Government possessed a "five to one superiority in combat troops and in rifles, a practical monopoly of heavy equipment and transport, and an unopposed air arm." *China White Paper*, 1949, p. 311.

31. Vinacke, *op. cit.*, p. 658.

32. *China White Paper*, 1949, pp. 607-609.

33. "Post-war Politics of China," P. M. A. Linebarger, in "Postwar Governments of the Far East," *Journal of Politics*, November, 1947, pp. 535-536.

34. *China White Paper*, 1949, p. 686.

35. The texts of the Yalta Agreements and the Sino-Soviet Treaty are in *China White Paper*, 1949, pp. 583-596.

36. *China White Paper*, 1949, pp. 596-597.

37. Vinacke, p. 673.

38. Vinacke, pp. 748-749.

39. *Korea, 1945-1948*, Department of State, Publication 3305, Far Eastern Series 28, p. 3.

40. George M. McCune, "Korea: The First Year of Liberation," *Pacific Affairs*, March, 1947, p. 8.

41. *Ibid.*

42. Vinacke, p. 751.

43. McCune, *loc. cit.*, p. 7.

44. Vinacke, pp. 751-752.

45. The Soviet representatives abstained from voting on the resolution.

46. U. S. Department of State, *Occupation of Japan: Policy and Progress*, Far Eastern Series No. 17, p. 7.

47. "United States Initial Post-Surrender Policy for Japan," *ibid.*, pp. 75-76.

48. Vinacke, pp. 745-746.

49. "United States Initial Post-Surrender Policy for Japan," *op. cit.*

50. Vinacke, p. 745.

51. *United States in World Affairs, 1947-1948,* Council on Foreign Relations, Harper, New York, 1948, pp. 8-9.

52. *Military Situation in the Far East, Hearings before the Committee on Armed Services and the Committee on Foreign Relations, U.S. Senate,* 82nd Congress, 1st Session, pt. 1, p. 18. Hereafter cited as *Hearings.*

53. *Hearings,* pt. 2, p. 759.

54. *Hearings,* pt. 2, p. 737.

55. *Hearings,* pt. 3, p. 1728. The exception was the International Postal Union, where the vote was later reversed.

56. *Hearings,* pt. 3, p. 1935.

57. Quoted in *Hearings,* pt. 1, p. 655.

58. *New York Times,* April 11, 1951, p. E3.

59. Text in *New York Times,* April 20, 1951. The quotations from General MacArthur which appear below are from this speech, unless otherwise indicated.

60. *Hearings,* pt. 2, p. 731.

61. *Hearings,* pt. 2, p. 732.

62. *Hearings,* pt. 1, p. 325.

62a. In the press report of his speech to Congress this reads: ". . . operation against the Chinese mainland." This was an error in recording, according to General MacArthur. See *New York Times,* May 5, 1951.

63. Secretary Acheson put it succinctly: "The objective of our military operation in Korea is to end the aggression, to safeguard against its renewal, and to restore peace." *Hearings,* pt. 3, p. 1717.

64. Secretary Acheson told the Joint Senate Committee: "We should also analyze the effect on our allies of our taking steps to initiate the spread of war beyond Korea. It would severely weaken their ties with us and in some instances it might sever them. . . . In relation to the total world threat, our safety requires that we strengthen, not weaken, the bonds of our collective-security system. The power of our coalition to deter an attack depends in part upon the will and confidence of our partners. If we, by the measures proposed, were to weaken that effect, particularly in the North Atlantic area, we would be jeopardizing the security of an area which is vital to our own national security." *Hearings,* pt. 3, p. 1719.

65. Thus neither is apt to view with satisfaction the proposed text of the Japan treaty, which (Ch. 2, Art. 1, b) reads: "Japan renounces all right, title and claim to Formosa and the Pescadores," but not specifically in favor of China. Text, *New York Times,* July 13, 1951, p. 4.

66. On this issue see the background statement in the controversial *Policy Information Paper, Formosa,* Special Guidance #28. Text in Hearings, pt. 3, pp. 1667-1669.

67.   The President's point of view, as stated by Secretary Acheson, was: "that we are not prejudicing the future of Formosa. That is a matter which should be decided . . . either in connection with the Japanese peace treaty or by the United Nations." *Hearings*, pt. 3, p. 1729.

68.   From General Marshall's testimony before the Senate Joint Committee, *Hearings*, pt. 1, p. 368-9.

69.   *Hearings*, pt. 1, pp. 23-4.

70.   *Hearings*, pt. 1, p. 24.

71.   Quotations from the draft text of this agreement and the Japanese treaty are from the *New York Times*, July 13, 1951, p. 4.

Index